CANADIAN BORDER

I-chi
hi fic
form
Peo of T
1972
L. hs

CONTINENTAL DIVIDE

Bear Paw
Sept. 30–Oct. 5

Col. Miles' Route

Cow Island
Sept. 23

• Lewistown

• Helena

Crows and
Bannocks

Butte •

Canyon Creek
Sept. 13

Big Hole
Aug. 9

• Virginia City

Yellowstone
Park

Howard's Route

Camas Meadows
Aug. 20

People of the Dream

BY JAMES FORMAN

The Skies of Crete
Ring the Judas Bell
The Shield of Achilles
Horses of Anger
The Traitors
The Cow Neck Rebels
So Ends This Day
Song of Jubilee
People of the Dream

People of the Dream

JAMES FORMAN

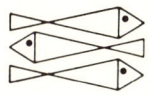

FARRAR, STRAUS & GIROUX   NEW YORK

Copyright © 1972 by James Forman
All rights reserved
First printing, 1972
Library of Congress catalog card number: 76-188271
ISBN 0-374-35804-4
Published simultaneously in Canada by Doubleday Canada Ltd., Toronto
Printed in the United States of America
Designed by Cynthia Basil

This one is for Joseph
and his people
and for Mary and her four boys,
particularly Chris,
who likes to see his name in print

Contents

I   Coming of the White Men   3
II   One-Armed Howard   29
III   First Blood   61
IV   In White Bird Canyon   75
V   The Clearwater   87
VI   The Bitterroots   108
VII   The Big Hole   129
VIII   The Long Retreat   152
IX   The Yellowstone   164
X   Cow Island   180
XI   The Camp at Bear Paw   187
XII   Death at Bear Paw   199
XIII   No Promised Land   214

People of the Dream

I
Coming of the White Men

It was in the early spring following his eighth winter that the boy went looking for visions and a name. The white men had baptized him and called him Ephraim, but that was their name, not his own. His people called him simply Little Turtle, but that was not a man's name. So he departed, leaving his lodge and his friends and the black dog who always wanted to follow.

Only the old man went with him, Red Grizzly Bear, the medicine talker, the man of tribal memories. Red Grizzly Bear was wrinkled and dark as venison smoked over the coals, but he still wore eagle feathers in his rivery white hair and carried a bow fashioned from the curled horns of the mountain sheep, though he could no longer draw it. He did not own a trader's gun, for he had always refused the white man's weapon even in his warrior days. He took only their beads and trinkets, working them into his buckskin shirt along with the teeth of the grizzly bear and the cured thumbs and forefingers of enemies he had slain in bygone battles. Red Grizzly Bear had tales to tell of those old days as they strode down the lava-rimmed canyon floor toward the great lake.

The deep eroded gorges of the Wallowa had always been the boy's winter home. In the mountains the snows piled higher than a man's head, so that a traveling brave had to use snowshoes, but in the gorges the snow never came. The grass stayed green; there was no danger of the ponies and the cattle starving. Not until spring did the boy's people climb up from the gorges and wander with their stock after the new grass. On either side rose pine-forested foothills, often shrouded in mist at that time of year. The surrounding mountains were entirely lost from view. Later in the spring the tribe would move down the valley toward the sparkling lake for the early-summer salmon fishing. Full summer saw them roving into the hills toward the mountains, which would now be clear beneath a friendly sun. There they would gather berries for winter, and hunt the deer until the leaves fell and the mist returned. When the wind howled once more from the west and the grass died, they would return to the haven of the canyons. So it had always been in the life of the boy and his people.

Now both the boy and the medicine talker were looking for a Wyakin, a spirit friend from the forest or the lake. The boy had never had such a friend. Red Grizzly Bear had many guardians, but now he was old, his wives were dead, and the winters were colder than they had been. He could use more help. He would instruct the boy that first night.

They camped in a beaver meadow of scattered willow clumps and good grass that bordered the stream where it emptied into the lake. The boy made a fire while the old man fished with a short spear. The light was fading rapidly when he returned with two small fish. They squatted close to the fire while the fish cooked, for it was growing cool and the smoke kept the mosquitoes away.

The boy had heard that one should never eat on a vision quest, and he did not touch the food, until the old man told him to. The next day, when he was alone, he could go without. Meanwhile, the old man was hungry, and with him it made no difference: whether he was hungry or full, the visions would come at his bidding.

When they had finished, the boy waited with interest for the summoning, but the medicine talker seemed to have forgotten about visions. He talked of the great warrior, Coyote, who had made the tribe out of the heart's blood of a monster slain in battle by a flint-tipped arrow. The old man's worn and fissured hands played in the air as he talked. He told how it had been when he was a boy: trips on horseback toward the sun's rising and the buffalo plains; toward its setting, where he'd traded with the bandy-legged Chinookans, who plied their shovel-nosed dugouts on the wide water. They smelled always of fish, and they flattened their babies' heads for nobility and thrust seashells through their noses for fierceness, though they were not really fierce. Once their own Nimpau people had used shells in this way, said Red Grizzly Bear, but no more, though the white man still called them Nez Percé, meaning the Pierced Noses.

The old man fell into singsong, grunting verse, recalling the dead days of his glory: skirmishes with the Shoshonis and the Crow, and the battle of Pierre's Hole, where he'd killed two Gros Ventres and taken their fingers before a bullet had found him. He'd suffered long with that wound. He'd earned a new name, Rotten

Belly, for the way it had festered. But he had survived, and claimed to this day that he could swallow smoke and make it come out through the bullet hole. Finally he talked of his dead wife Watkuweis, who had guided the big blades, Lewis and Clark, through their valley. They had come needing help and had received it. For this they had returned gifts: iron arrowheads, kettles, a strong medicine to cure blindness, and the first guns. The finest gift of all had been Clark's son, born to a squaw in the springtime of their departure. It had gone well on both sides, this meeting with the white man, but that was over forty winters ago. All the white men brought with them now was whiskey and smallpox.

The Sunbearer rested a moment on the lip of the western mountains, then vanished, leaving a glow that soon was overmatched by the small fire. A full moon began rising hand over fist, and the boy and the medicine talker were hushed and silent at the beauty of her coming. There was no sound except the lapping of the water until, joltingly in that silence, a shot rang out. Its echo reverberated across the lake. White men? Only the white Bostons would do that. No Indian would fire at such a time. Even the beast he might presently be eating had a right to such a moment.

"The bow is more silent, the arrow quicker, grandson," observed the old warrior, who had so often played the arrow game, putting eight arrows into flight before the first could touch the ground. Eight arrows! Swifter than the swallow. The boy could almost see them golden against the last light. Another shot rolled away. Then the darkness and the night took over. A mule deer passed, quiet as a shadow, to drink in the stream. He raised his head from the water, ears alert, jaws dripping, and saw them. He vanished as elusive as smoke. "I could have shot him," said Red Grizzly Bear, but he had not even touched the bow. They were well fed. Why, then, offend the deer's spirit and kill him for nothing?

Around the curve of the lake, another campfire glowed. "I should find out who they are," said Red Grizzly Bear, but he did not move. "I am quickly tired. My voice and limbs tremble."

"I will go for you, grandfather," the boy offered, but the old man said it was better to scatter the fire. They would be safe then. He had the bow, which neither he nor the boy could draw, and he had his many Wyakins, who would guard them in the dark.

The boy lay still. He listened to the insect voices and to the whispering of the water as it traveled from higher places. He thought of where the river was born in the high country of small lakes, stony cliffs, and ice, and he imagined pine-chip canoes swirling away, farther than he had ever been. He felt no desire to follow them, yet he felt a springtime well-being in his heart. This was good. This was beautiful. He would stay awake throughout the night; but long before the dawn, he slept.

The sun was high in the trees before Red Grizzly Bear awakened him. The old man had seen a stag with one great antler only, very strange, very majestic. Whether it had come in fact or in dreams he did not know or care, but it was his new Wyakin. The boy felt a pang. He had seen nothing, and now the old man would eat and then he would go home. There remained time only for brief instruction. Inexperienced as he was, he would be more likely to catch a vision if he did not eat or sleep. A plunge into the icy lake might help. Red Grizzly Bear recommended all this, and he told how a boy's Wyakin might take many forms: a deer illuminated in sudden lightning, a grizzly standing on a precipice with the Sunbearer flaming behind him. So it had been with the old man and from this sign he had taken his name, knowing that from then on in times of trouble he and the bear were brothers. The boy would know. A coyote Wyakin would give him cunning; a deer, speed of foot. It was something a boy must find for himself. But if it were no true vision—should he take a name out of pure fancy without a sign being given, then he would have no friend in nature, but a mortal enemy.

So the old man left him there. He went slowly, not looking back, and the boy watched him. He did not think the new Wyakin would be much help to Red Grizzly Bear or that all his Wyakins would see him through another winter. Then the boy was alone. He was no stranger to this world and he looked with calm eyes at his sisters, the busy birds, and his brother the black squirrel. To climb that way, to fly! A raccoon came to hunt frogs at the water's edge. Later a mule deer passed, his white rump and black tail a perfect target. Seeing no danger in the unarmed boy, the deer browsed for grass and mushrooms in the beaver meadow. Having no one else to talk to, the boy sang about the deer and about Dawn's house, and the coming of he-rain. Slowly the sun moved west. Many creatures came and went. The clouds made pictures, but there was no vision. At the boy's feet little black ants moved in single file, working and wrestling a dead beetle, scrabbling this way and that. "Work together," he told them. "All together." Then he sang a song softly to the setting sun and the coming dark, and because of his own voice he could not be sure what sound he heard. It seemed like laughter, still far away. After that he did not sing. He sank into the shadows by the stream and listened. The fish rising to the surface made soft sounds like drops of rain in dark pools. Then a beaver swam downstream, startling the fish. Close to the bank he paused, seemed intent upon something, then plunged back, thrashing, into the water. He swam frantically in a tight circle as though some water spirit had him by the leg, then finally he vanished. The boy wondered if indeed he had seen a vision, but it seemed evil somehow. He did not want to think he had seen an evil spirit at work, and he knew nothing of underwater traps.

"A boy does not turn into a brave overnight," he told himself, repeating his father's words to give himself courage. It took patience and growing. Mostly it took time. He waited. By now the moon was up, full, high, and pale. A shred of cloud topped it like a war bonnet. This was not a good enough vision either. Taking Red Grizzly Bear's advice, the boy shed his breechcloth and moccasins and stepped naked into the stream. Then he plunged, and the cold of that mountain stream shot needles into his flesh and took his breath away.

He scrambled out, gasping.

Laughter stopped him short, almost drove him back into the water. They had come from nowhere, two dark and brooding figures, tall and broad, and for a moment he thought they were the Old Man and his brother from up the river, those imaginary ogres of his childhood. But these two were real enough and far more dangerous than stories. The bigger one grabbed him by the hair and almost jerked him off his feet. "Been stealing beaver, have you?" he said in the Chinook jargon, which was the trade talk up and down these rivers. "Turn them over, or it'll go hard with you."

The boy, who had never hunted anything but fish, who belonged to a tribe to whom the thought of trapping beaver for their skins alone was repellent, only lowered his face.

"Red Belly, I'm talking to you. Where's the beaver?" As he spoke, the white man cocked an enormous brown paw, then struck a short blow which flung the boy to the ground. Then he was jerked up again. He kept his eyes closed, but he did not speak or cry out as another blow caught him high on the cheek, then on the nose. When he fell flat on his face, he felt a foot glance along his ribs. But he had taken the hot coals from the lodge fire and held them in his hand to know pain and to stand it, and he would not have uttered a sound if the man had kicked him to death. He might have, too, if the other, wallowing in the water, hadn't shouted: "Lay off, Jim.

I've got it. "And he hauled out onto the bank the almost shapeless lump of a drowned beaver. A steel trap affixed to both hind legs gave off a dull glint in the moonlight.

"Let the Indian go, Jim. He's only a whippersnapper."

"What about the other traps, then? What about them, boy?" The big man leaned very close, showing yellow teeth and a glittering eye. He seemed to be winking; Little Turtle could not make out his other eye. And his breath was bad—sweet, sickening, and thick. "Better lug him along to the camp, Matt. His scalp might come in handy to patch my britches." The trapper laughed and all the while kept his hand clamped on the boy's neck.

"Struggle, and like as not you'll end up throttled," he said. "Now march along, Red Belly."

So the three of them crossed the stream, mounted the far bank, and went in among the trees. A great cloud had covered the moon. In the darkness the trapper called Jim blundered into a tree and lost his grip on the boy. Little Turtle spun free, only to be caught by the ankle.

"Let the boy go," urged the other trapper. "What do we want with him?"

"He's coming!"

The rest of the way, Little Turtle was dragged by the foot. Fortunately, it wasn't far. By the time the moon had fully reappeared, they had reached the camp. Clearly the pair had been trapping the lake for some time, for they had built a skin lodge and from the trees hung many pelts pressed flat into bundles. To one side were the pale naked bodies of stripped beaver, their stomachs blown up with gas and their flesh sequined with sated flies. The man called Matt stirred up the coals from a glow into bright fire. Jim sat down Indian-fashion. He forced the boy to sit beside him and tied his wrists with a rawhide strap. "Don't move," he said, fishing for something in a deep pocket. It was a bottle, green and lovely. If he had had anything to trade, if he hadn't been so afraid, Little Turtle would have bargained for it. He watched, fascinated, as the cork came out. The bottle went to the man's lips and the contents went down, the man's Adam's apple bobbing beneath his beard with each swallow.

"You'd like some, wouldn't you? You Redskins all love it."

The white man grinned. His square yellow teeth protruded, giving his mouth the look of laughter even when he wasn't laughing. Little Turtle was reminded of a grizzly bear somehow stuffed into buckskin, an old battler with scars to show. A long white one ran from scalp to beard, and a gouged-out eye had left behind nothing but a raw socket. He had victories, too, judging by the scalps at his belt; Indian scalps, unless he only murdered women with long black hair.

While Jim drank, Little Turtle watched. The man named Matt was busy preparing the beaver. First the tail, the only palatable part, came off for eating. Then he cut along the belly and down each leg, peeling the heavy pelt back and off. It went onto a willow hoop for drying and stretching, and the naked corpse joined its fellows. Then the inner tail went over the fire, along with a rabbit. Little Turtle hadn't eaten for a day and part of a night. He felt hunger despite himself.

They gave him no food. The men ate, talked Boston talk he could not understand, seemed to quarrel. Jim ended up saying in Chinook: "Ever fight twelve drunken Indians?"

"No. But I'd like to see it done. Hell, it's your booze. You waste it."

Jim turned back to Little Turtle. His expression remained the same, but his one eye narrowed as a cat's does in strong light. He gave a juicy laugh. "I'm going to give you a treat, boy; get you started early. Your daddy'd give his eyeteeth for a slug of this whiskey, and all you got to do is say 'Please.'" Little Turtle was confused. He didn't understand half of what the man had said. He only knew that the bottle was being pushed his way, and that the man who seemed to be playing wasn't playing at all. He was a killer; it was in his eye. When the boy didn't take the bottle, the man forced it on him and made him drink. He choked. Tears came to his eyes, and all the while Jim watched, chewing, his one eye secret, serene, and deadly.

"Leave off, Jim. Let him be. He's just a young'un," said the other.

Jim forced the bottle toward Little Turtle again. "Drink," he ordered.

"Jim, when you've been drinking, you can get as mean as cat dung and twice as nasty. Leave him be."

"Now listen here, Matt. Whiskey peddlers are the advance guard of civilization. That's the damned truth.

You know it. And it's a damn sight better way for the old Redskin to go and a sight less trouble than having to take his scalp. I'd give him a hoe if I thought he'd hang onto it. Don't matter much. One way or another, it's making these here mountains safe for democracy. I'm just helping things along."

"Leave off, Jim. I'm telling you."

"You ain't big enough for that, Matt. No, you ain't." For emphasis Jim spat into the fire as straight and hard as though he'd used a blowpipe. "Mind your own business, Matt, old friend. You're the one who said I'd cut a fellow's throat twice for a dollar, and for four bits I'd lick the cut clean. Well, I just might."

Matt stood up. His nostrils seemed to have pinched in. His ears moved back like a wolf's. Little Turtle watched warily. Jim stood up, too—or half stood up, in a crouching way which reminded Little Turtle of a mountain lion he had once seen the braves bring home. The first contact was more of a slap, it seemed to Little Turtle. Matt gave it. He was the quicker as they circled, facing each other. It looked like a rough game they'd played before, but Jim's one eye was dour and red as a grizzly's. He tried a fierce blow to Matt's body and missed. Matt fended him off with the freshly killed beaver, a kind of limp club. He got in a good lick with it and then suddenly they were close, exchanging fierce blows to the body, neither one giving an inch.

Little Turtle edged toward the trees. Somewhere he might hide in the lap of his mother the earth, but the whiskey burned in his empty stomach and the air whirled when he tried to walk.

Behind him the game was over. He had not seen it happen, but first one, then the other, had drawn a knife. "Quit it! That's enough, Jim. You're drunk, for God's sake!" Matt shouted, as he backed off. "You win. You win. Scalp the kid if you want. Don't come at me, Jim!"

Jim kept coming, slow and certain. Matt turned his back for an instant and made a dash for his saddlebags. Jim lumbered after, but not fast enough, for Matt had time to snatch out a big cap-and-ball revolver, long and heavy as a small rifle. Its hammer was cocked and ready. Jim pulled up short. He patted the air reassuringly. "Put away the bowie, Jim." He slipped the knife into his belt. "Now go on back and sit down. Cool off and keep your hands off that bottle, hear?" Jim did everything he was told. He almost sauntered and then, quick as a bear salmon-fishing, his hands shot out. He crouched, turned, and the striped rifle which until that moment had been leaning against a tree went off. Matt looked surprised. His knees sagged. He fumbled for his chest and at the same time toppled forward, his arms and the pistol crumpled under him. The shot echoed away through the forest.

Silence.

"Matt?" Jim said. "Hey, Matt. Get on up . . . Matt? Oh, my God." He lumbered to his companion and knelt over him. "Oh, God, Matt. Why'd you provoke me? You provoked me, Matt. I didn't . . . That damned

Indian." He looked wildly around, but the fire gave little light and an obscuring mist was rising from the lake. He found the green bottle, hurled it into the thickets. "You damned Indian!" He began beating through the bushes, using his rifle as a club. He thrashed the saplings until the stock broke off, then staggered on, crashing through the trees. For some time Little Turtle could hear him, and then it was still. Somewhere from the mountainside a cougar gave its kill cry in the night. It sounded like the scream of a frightened woman. Little Turtle was alone again. Mosquitoes hummed in swarms about his face, but his flesh was numb and did not feel them. Inside his brain the horror stood out as sharp as bright beadwork. Finally even this was dulled by exhaustion and the fuming whiskey. Before the moon set, his aunt the night took him with her cool hands. Little Turtle, whom some called Young Joseph after his father, slept with his wrists bound, and his dreams were of the white man and of days spent at the mission at Lapwai.

He had gone with his father for the big prayer medicine of the whites. He had seen with awe the black book of the white man, the powerful medicine. "What a friend we have in Jesus, all our sins and griefs to bear. What a privilege to carry everything to God in prayer." He and his father had learned the prayers, and they had been baptized by Reverend Spalding. Ephraim, they had called him, though he was still Little Turtle among the Nez Percé, with no deeds or Wyakin to his name. He remembered in his dream how it had ended, a year ago. Some had said the missionaries were bringing in Bostons to take the Indian land away, and then the Cayuses had risen up against their missionary, Marcus Whitman, and slain him. Little Turtle saw it all now in bloody visions: Joe Louis the half-breed maverick with his woman dead of the white man's pox; Joe Louis bringing down his flimsy pipe tomahawk on the back of Whitman's head, then cutting his throat. And he could see Whitman's woman, Narcissa, large and white—some called her beautiful—down on her knees beside her husband, praying, not even seeming to notice that she herself was shot in the arm. But they had taken her up and carried her outside on a sofa. "Stop, my children," she had admonished them. "This is a great sin which God will punish." Obediently they had stopped and set the sofa down and shot her twice as she tried to rise. Then, because she was so white, they had rolled her in the mud.

It was a bad thing, which even children remember in nightmares from the telling, and Little Turtle and his father Joseph had not returned again to Lapwai. He had seen no other whites until this night, and he wished to see no more.

Dawn Boy, the little chief, aroused him with a soft touch. It came back slowly: the trappers, the fight, part of a dream memory. He had dreamed it all, along with the Whitman massacre. But then he saw the body, face down by the still-smoldering fire. There seemed to be a tomahawk planted deep in his own skull as he stood up. He shook his head as though to dislodge the pain, and that made it worse. The last place he wanted to go was near that body and the ghost which must be lingering near; but a knife protruded from the corpse's belt and the boy's hands were still bound. He asked the ghost's permission, then cut the thongs, and returned the knife to the dead man, lest the spirit be offended.

Gradually the mist was shredding away as the sun probed down and the horizon began to draw back. Dark silhouettes of pines began to show on the slopes. Soon Day would come and the other Boston might return. He could not linger there, though he took the charred beaver tail from the fire. There was dry flesh on it still, and nourishment. The sun flamed in the sky. Hurry, he told himself, there is no time. Little Turtle left the clearing. He took nothing with him, until he came upon the green bottle of the night before. This he picked up because it was beautiful. He would keep it. He didn't know why. He wasn't even sure whether he should laugh or cry. He wanted to do one or the other, but neither was common to his people, who would shout or sing or, more often, keep silent.

He had to cross the stream where he and Red Grizzly Bear had camped. The sun warmed the surface and drew off spirals of mist. Great misty rings, as if drawn from some shaman's pipe, floated lazily above the water. "I might catch a fish," he thought. He remembered the great ritual fish hunts when the salmon first ran and how the water turned thick with them, darting, sliding, leaping above the surface as the fishermen slapped the water. He thought how it was to wait, mouth watering, while the medicine man roasted and ate the first fish, honoring it with the delicacy of the procedure and returning its bones to the water so that the others would not mind being taken. His stomach contracted now at the thought of fresh salmon, but there was no time. Luckily, he found his clothes where he had left them. Then he plunged in and paddled across, feeling clean and refreshed when he stepped out on the other side, his moccasins oozing water. Morning was a good time. Softly he sang the song to the rising sun as he went along.

After a while he grew tired. "I am sick," he told himself. "I will sing the song for making me well." But he still felt sick and he yearned for the lodge and his family and the brew of black and white roots which his mother would make. Still, he was alive, and he thanked the sky and the earth and the four corners of the world for that. By midmorning he did find some of the crimson hearts which white men called strawberries, but they were not ripe and he threw them up. For a while he rested. It was not far now, and when he knew that he could walk into camp without showing weakness he went the rest of the way. They asked him about his face when he arrived. He told them that he had fallen and that he had seen no vision, for truly there was no Wyakin in what he had seen.

Only his younger brother heard everything. He could never keep anything from Ollokot, who had the liveliest and most honest eyes one could hope to see. Ollokot had addressed him seriously, the way men talked in council. "Grandfather, you are different. If you saw no vision, you saw something."

"I saw the big blades," he admitted.

"Yes?"

And so he told, going over it three times to prove that it was true, for that was the Nez Percé way. When Ollokot finally knew that what he heard was more than a story, he said, "Ayee! I would have fought them. I would have taken their scalps."

Little Turtle made a gesture of brushing aside, "With a toy arrow, grandfather?"

Then Ollokot nodded, grinning, so that Little Turtle could not keep himself from smiling back. But that was all right between brothers. Finally he showed Ollokot the green bottle. "Ayee . . . better than a scalp." Ollokot held it up toward Father Sun, who smiled upon them. The bottle glowed and Little Turtle could see the excitement in Ollokot's eyes and feel the warmth in his own.

"Grandfather," he said—the old joke had become a way of address between them—"the bottle is yours."

"Ayeee! The beauty of it!"

Little Turtle went out alone for visions in the years that followed. He went alone, for he was no longer a child, and Red Grizzly Bear had died that winter with his hands full of Wyakins. On these trips Little Turtle saw birds in flight and the beasts of the forest, but nothing that was worthy of a chief's son, a chief-to-be. They called him Young Joseph now. He stood six feet tall and more, and was built like a wrestler. His face was broad, an open, honest face full of kindness and dignity which even the white man trusted. There was in every life a time to be weaned, a time to be borne on the cradle board, a time to walk with the women and with the men, and a time to walk alone.

In the white man's reckoning, it was the summer of 1863. The white tribes were at war far away, so the story went, but that did not keep them from interfering with the Indians. A brave should look only to the moment, the day at hand, but Young Joseph, though he was strong and confident, felt a sadness at the heart of things, for he sensed something new in his valley. Few whites had come, yet he had seen the distant caravans and had heard the talk at Lapwai of gold and of good grass for the taking. Few whites had come, but something, some change, was already here. There were the huts along the Salmon River, springing up like toadstools in the night. There had been the big powwow at Lapwai. His father and Old James Red Wolf, all the chiefs of the Nez Percé, and many warriors had gone, riding two abreast, their faces painted, their ponies beaded and plumed. They had made a fine show of beating drums and brandished shields. Then in the great canvas tent they had settled down to talk. It was there that the white man always won. The whites had offered, then demanded, to buy most of the land set aside by the Treaty of 1855, leaving for the Nez Percé only the settled land around Lapwai. The Indians who already lived at Lapwai were led by Lawyer, who wore cast-off white man's clothes and leather shoes. Those Indians went to church on Sunday and tore the skin of their mother the earth with the white man's hoe. They had lost their nobility. They were no longer Indians.

For days the talk had gone on. No matter the old treaties, the old laws. What was not legal one day could be made so the next by the Army. Some of the Nez Percé held out. Others gave way. Big Thunder, who had seen already eighty winters, said finally, "I am very sick. I am spitting blood. Excuse me." And he had gone home to die. Even Kamiakin capitulated, saying, "I am tired of talk. I am anxious to go back to my garden." In the end Lawyer had signed, and with him the other Lapwai chiefs whose land was within the proposed reservation. Old Joseph, who would lose the Wallowa under the new paper, signed nothing and took no gifts, but turned his back on the conference tent and rode home wearing his war paint.

He was an old man when he finally spoke with his son, old except for his eyes, which were the color of the mountains, stormy and unvanquished. "The whites say it is for our good that we move, that they will protect us from the settlers and give us schools. They want to pay us with whistles and shoestrings." He spat on the ground. "Yes. The Boston spit in our faces and we say it is raining. Lawyer and his kind are bad. They smell like death. I don't hate them. The Bostons have made them that way. Grandson"—even a father addressed his own son in this way—"hear me and remember. We are made of soil and water. Everything on this earth is made of soil and water. We do not own any part of the earth. We are part of it, and cannot sell what we do not own.

We are part of the Wallowa forever. Never forget that."

It was with such thoughts and dawning responsibilities in mind that Young Joseph set out for the fifth time on a spirit quest. Always before, he had gone down the canyon to the lake, but this time he went up past tumbling waters. His objective was the mountains. It seemed a good omen that a golden eagle circled high above on great tilting wings, gliding off in huge circles, curving back. Young Joseph yearned for the eagle as a spirit friend. To be an eagle was to be above everything, seeing all, soaring through mountain gorges, rising to the snowy peaks. Even when he plunged to the deepest canyon in his lowest glide, the eagle was higher than other birds.

Out of the canyon, Joseph crossed the plateau with its willows and cottonwood groves where snakes coiled in the lava outcroppings. He pushed through bunch grass, avoiding the whir of a rattler, and kept on, always gaining height toward the forested domain of the elk and the bear and the horned sheep.

Toward dusk he made his camp at the pass that led from Wallowa to Lapwai and the fort. He had not been to the spot since his father's return from the big pow-wow. With his brother, Ollokot, he had met their father there. The old man had taken out the sacred Bible before them and ripped out pages by the handful and scattered them, great snowflakes on the wind. He had looked tired and beaten. "Their heaven is too high for me. Our valley is good enough," he had said. "The whites may need a book to teach them good and bad, but I need it no longer. 'The Lord giveth and taketh.' With Indians it is always 'Taketh.' They get us down on our knees praying while behind the hill they dig their mines into the earth. Behind our backs they are building cabins and running off our ponies." To Young Joseph this seemed a rash act; the dying figure on the cross had always held him in awe. But he was a cruel God to pay with blood for blood.

"Christ died for all men," Young Joseph said, remembering the lesson.

"Not for the Indian," said his father. "You are young. You won't listen." And he cursed the white man's god and put him away, content with the Great Spirit, who, even if he was hard upon them, left them the land of their birth and did not send them in death to deep fires below. All true, and yet for Young Joseph there was something impelling about the white man's god. "Love your enemy," he had said, and such a love must be unbelievably strong.

With the book scattered, Old Joseph directed his sons to gather up stones to make piles marking the boundary of his land. That was the white man's way, which they could understand. They went about the task grimly, marking out the earth in this manner, while the old man harangued them. "I have done much for my people," he said. "Now I am old. You must support me. When my bones creak, you must bring me venison and bear's oil. When the ashes of life cool, you must bring fire, and when I die, you must bury me in this valley and look after the people."

For two days they had piled up the stones, and then it was done: our land and theirs. Perhaps it was wise, Young Joseph thought—perhaps, if the whites paid any attention. But Ollokot, who would be the tribe's war leader one day, felt caged. It was against everything he believed and even against what their father had said. But he could think of no better way.

The stones still stood and Joseph camped by them now. The pages from the book were gone. He made no fire, as it was a warm night and he had nothing to eat. The stone cairns looked like tombstones under the moon. With the first trace of dawn, he set out through somber pines and cottonwood, where the deer lived and the bears and the cougars, where the beaver hid in icy winter streams. He followed the wolves' paths, crossing the mountain at the lower ridges, and then took the shorter, steeper paths made by the deer. Still high above, the crests rose blue and soft, becoming darker and knife-edged as he approached them. Now he was a visitor in sacred ground, the domain of the old gods, for the mountains of the world are old, but the mountains of his own country seemed the oldest.

In mid-afternoon he emerged above the tree line into the refuge of the eagle and the thundercloud. He followed a trickle of icy water upward to its source, the stone from which it would spring unfailingly until the Great Spirit of those mountains decreed that its years had run out. Now the Sunbearer sank behind the peaks and thrust down a long shadow arm into the land he loved. The wind whispered. Taking no food and only a sip of water, Joseph sat down by the stream to wait and watch. The dark hours passed uneventfully. Thoughts swam through his brain like silver fish, but there were no visions. With the new day a herd of elk came down to drink. They sparred and frolicked, following one another in a tight circle, a game about which Joseph had only heard stories. That was good. He was seeing the world as it once had been, before the white man, perhaps before the Indian. Though he had passed a night without sleep or visions, his spirits rose, and he tilted his head back to see the mountains and the warming friendly sky. Ranges piled up one upon another, the great unknown country. Then he looked down on the earth, the mother from whom he had come, to whom he would return. What he could not see in fact he saw with his mind: the whole of the Wallowa unrolling, the deep gorges, the Snake River boiling in its rocky bed, the Powder River more of a woman, gentler. They were but silver threads in the distance, but he knew them as he knew his brothers, the forest trees, and the animals who dwelt there. He was forever part of it until death and after.

It was then that he saw them, figures almost too small to be real: three burros and two men, all black against the glitter of a stream bed far below. Joseph had heard about them at Oro Fino Creek and along the Salmon River. Gold miners. White men. First came the few with the pans, then the crowds with their sluices and sluice boxes dredging out the canyon walls, and then the towns.

He watched them moving up the bright snaking canyon, and as he watched, a darkness came into his heart and into the sky itself. Looking to the west where he thought the Great Spirit lived, he saw a cloud rolling up to brood over the mountains. Thunder muttered; a flutter of wind shook the air. Like a majestic ocean wave, the cloud line broke over the rocky peaks and flowed down. Blue-white scratches of lightning stroked the sky like the clawings of a giant bear. Swiftly the sky and the sun were engulfed. Darkness held the land, and there was a last silence before the storm broke. Lightning cut through the air. Voices seemed to come joyously through the drum beating of the rain, and Joseph cried aloud to the thunder, the cry of the loosed eagle, an abandonment to the storm and his god. The Great Spirit was everywhere, in everything that crawls and swims and flies. Amid that shouting, crashing din, he heard a great voice that came from everywhere. "Joseph, do not forsake them. They are your people." It did not happen as the missionary told of such things in the Bible, for the voice was inside him. But it did happen.

It rained still on the far side of the valley and everything was sharp and clear as seen through a magic lens. The river below was a torrent now. Joseph saw no signs of the miners, and he was happy—more than happy. He was a walking song. Whatever else happened, there would be nothing quite like this. With no sense of weariness or hunger, he started down. Above him hung the eagles, aloof couriers from the spirit world, but he recognized them. He felt the wonderful sameness of things, the unfailing way in which expectation was fulfilled. He knew in that moment the beautiful wild order of the world. From that moment on he had a Wyakin and a name: Thunder Traveling to Loftier Mountaintops. It was too glorious for normal use. History would remember him simply as Chief Joseph.

II
One-Armed Howard

It was the month when bears come out of hibernation; when the silence of the snow gives way to the music of water. The year was 1877, and the two tall chiefs stood face to face, solid as the mountains. Their faces were alike. Each man wore his hair swept high like the mane of a horse, then down his back in braids. That was the way of the men of the Dreamer faith, the new Indian religion. Only in their hands did they differ, for Joseph's were slender and sinewy and Ollokot's were thick and scarred, hardened by the bow and the hunt. The buckskin looked tight across his shoulders as if he had only to set his muscles to tear the seams apart.

"With my fist and your brain, brother, we will be all right," he said.

"No fighting with the white-eyes." Joseph spoke with the certainty of one who explains all with a single statement. "No fighting."

"What other way, brother?"

"You can never kill them all. They are like the grasshoppers in the prairies. We are few. We must save the lives of our people and shed no blood."

"Brother," Ollokot said, "cannot the greatest trouble sometimes come from trying to avoid trouble? Have not the whites pushed down our father's stones, and taken our cattle and built their wooden lodges on our land?"

"There can be no fighting," Joseph said again. "When

you start killing, it is like setting a fire on the plains. I have eyes and a heart. I can see that if we fight, we will have to leave all and go into the mountains. Now tell of the powwow, brother."

They had been called in for a powwow at Lapwai, but since One-Armed Howard was not to be present, Joseph had not gone. He would treat with no one less than General Howard, and so Ollokot had traveled with a burden of decision such as Joseph had never borne.

"We talked of peace," Ollokot said, "but all faces were black with war. They want our Wallowa, our valley. They tell us to go to Lapwai forever. They will pay."

"They did not pay the Cayuses. They did not pay Lawyer's people."

"I saw rapid-fire guns at the fort," Ollokot said.

"They only wait for us to do one bad thing, steal one horse, murder one white man, and they will have an excuse. I know," Joseph said. "Brother, tell me what was said, so that I may see it all."

So Ollokot told of it, and Joseph could see it clearly behind his eyes: the log houses at Lapwai, the great canvas tent set up, the soldiers in blue standing about uneasily, the Indians in their finery, some cowed into silence, others strutting. Toohoolhoolzote, the barrel-chested, broad-faced, high priest of the Dreamer's faith, had talked for the Nez Percé.

"The earth is part of my body," he had said. "I belong to the land out of which I came. The earth is my mother."

Then the soldiers replied with weary insistence. "We do not wish to interfere with your religion," they said, "but you must talk about practical things. Over and over you tell us the earth is your mother. Let us hear no more of that, but come to business."

Toohoolhoolzote spoke again, undaunted, his voice ringing: "You ask me to come to Lapwai. You ask me to plow the ground. Shall I take a knife and tear my mother's bosom? Then she will not take me to her bosom to rest. You ask me to dig for yellow stone. Shall I dig under her skin for her bones? Then I may not enter her body to be born again. You ask me to cut the grass and make hay and sell it and be rich like white men, but how dare I cut off my mother's hair?" So he went on, while the soldiers frowned, urged, and then threatened. He went on like a cornered bear, grimly turning his huge head this way and that. In the end they had taken Toohoolhoolzote away to jail.

"The whites do not listen," Ollokot said. "They draw lines on the earth that we cannot see and tell us not to cross them. They find ways of showing us that we are doing wrong when all we are doing is sitting still. They spoke of the Thieves' Treaty of '63, when Lawyer tried to sell our land. That Lawyer has left our ways. He walks in moccasins on the white man's road. He is rich, but his heart is empty."

"He has lost the trail of beauty," Joseph said. "We must pity him."

"The white men say we must come in soon and choose our reservation land before the white settlers get it all.

They are coming, grandfather. I counted on both hands the new lodges they have built. We live in freedom today; tomorrow on the reservation; the day after, in a cage."

"Did no one speak against this?" Joseph asked.

"What could we say? Five Crows said, 'We are tired.' He was right. There will be no more talk until you come. They say One-Armed Howard will be there."

"He is a fair man," Joseph replied, knowing that next time he would have to go. But how could he explain to the whites? They would understand less after he had tried. He had no right to make mistakes, to fail, and he knew it. The whites offered a comfortable life in their own way—a plot of land, tools, a church to attend. But to be shut away from the meadows and the sky he knew would be worse than the furnace in the Bible.

Joseph looked at Ollokot and saw without words that he understood, and his brother said as much without any words being spoken. They had been born in this valley. Their father was born and buried here, and his father, forever. The force that drove the spring floods through the canyons of the Wallowa drove the red blood through the veins of their people. The whites could tell them to go to another country, but here they were and here they must stay. Ollokot reached out both hands and grasped Joseph's. "All will be well, one day," he said.

"All will be well," Joseph echoed, "as long as we are together. We must never get hurt, either of us." There were tears in his eyes, and for a moment he believed that they had been given a sign. They would survive no matter what lay ahead, if only they clung together. All this was said without words, and the two chiefs embraced and wrestled and spoke loudly to each other.

Since their father had died, these two had led the tribe: Joseph in peace, Ollokot on the hunt and in war. Dead for six years, helpless for longer, Old Joseph was still with them in Young Joseph's thoughts and decisions. "I have but one last thing to teach you. Never give up your home. Never." And the son had promised. "That is well done," the old man had said, and after that, Young Joseph was chief in fact, though the old man still retained until his death the right of first comment. He no longer ruled except through the arms of his sons, for he was blind, and traveled only with his hand resting lightly on Young Joseph's wrist. It was as though he had said all there was to say and seen all there was to see, as though even before dying he had climbed out of this world into some higher calm.

Yet until the last he had ridden the valley with his sons. He'd weighed so little . . . Joseph remembered helping him onto his own pony and then climbing up behind as Ollokot swung onto his mount's back in one smooth motion as a warrior should. Then they would ride, checking the boundary stones. The brothers would sing a hunting song, their voices blending pleasantly in the harmony of old comradeship. But the old man rode in silence, never seeing the McCormack cabin, or the Keith herd, or the places being staked off by the Mastersons and Tulleys. Young Joseph knew all the settlers and had tried friendly persuasion to move them. When they would not go, he had accepted them unhappily and offered only friendship, so long as they kept to their end of the valley. And though they passed the new white settlement on these rides, Old Joseph remained unaware and spoke not a word. Still, Joseph suspected that he saw further somehow than the rest of them. Toward the last he must have seen the happy grounds beyond the stars as well as the white man's hell, for his father had had the eyes of one who was more than a man. They had been the eyes of a woman, too, and a shaman; that was his greatness. Now Joseph needed all his father's wisdom when it came to meeting with One-Armed Howard, for his tribe and his home valley, the Wallowa, were at stake.

Until now Joseph had refused to take action, but those days of indecision were ending. In the few that remained, he went to the forest edge, where he talked with the dead. When the day of departure came, he put on his best buckskin, milk-tanned, white, and soft as velvet. There were no beads or porcupine-quill decorations on his moccasins and leggings, no feathers in his hair, no weapons. But he was the chief, plain enough. Ollokot rode beside him, dressed much the same, though he carried a Winchester carbine in a beaded scabbard. The braves rode behind them in single file, and then some of the squaws. Joseph's wife did not come. She was great with child and must keep apart, but his daughter, Spring Song, wild and free as her name, rode with them on an appaloosa.

Along the way they were joined by other chiefs with

their people. First came Toohoolhoolzote, the medicine talker who had been taken captive during the last pow-wow and later released. He had known sixty-eight winters and the lines of his nose to the corners of his mouth were severe and chiseled as mountain granite. His soul was just as unmovable. For years he had been chief spokesman for the non-treaty Nez Percé, those who had entered into no agreement with the whites. As high priest of the Dreamer faith, which called upon the Indians to return to the old, pure ways, he loathed the whites and their Christianity. Joseph feared Toohoolhoolzote. He feared his trance-like silences. Even more he feared his ravings, when his eyes became two crazed and burning crystals, for in this visionary there was explosive fury that could bring disaster on them all.

Joining them that same day was Looking Glass, who bore his father's name for the mirror he wore around his neck. He looked gaudy on his painted gray traveling horse with his soldier's hat trimmed with otter fur. Some took him for a clown, but there was power in the brown swell of his forearms, and authority rested lightly on his broad shoulders. No talker, but tough and brutish as a grizzly at bay, Looking Glass appeared ready at any instant to raise the war whoop. He had never lost a fight, and in this alone there was reassurance. No visions clouded his judgment, and Joseph knew Looking Glass would restrain himself in counsel with the whites if the whites did not try to steal his pride.

Oldest chief of the non-treaties was White Bird. He joined them on the last day of the journey to Lapwai.

White Bird, a shaman and civil leader from the Salmon River country, bore the eagle wing, sign of a medicine man. His face was lean and his fierce hooked nose had a cutting edge, but his warrior days were done. He rode now hunched and silent, his blanket drawn tight against the wind. Joseph knew White Bird longed for peace like a veteran bull moose which has snapped its antlers in furious combat. White Bird was too old for war. His pleasures were in the lodge fires, the warm closeness of his fat squaw, old, safe stories. He would be cautious in his talking with the whites. He wished no trouble, only to be left alone.

On the morning of the council, they rode onto the Lapwai Reservation. The treaty Nez Percé, standing below the stockade wall, watched them pass. Looking Glass and White Bird looked proudly straight ahead. They were on show now. Toohoolhoolzote followed, his eyes closed as though in a dream. At the end rode Joseph. Fearing an incident, he riveted his attention on the mixed band of warriors. The braves, stripped to their war clouts, painted, plumed, their horses dabbed white and crimson, rode single-file, a grand show, stirring wistful memories in the hearts of the watching treaty Nez Percé.

Before they reached the camping ground, they were met by Reuben, a reservation Indian who spoke the white man's tongue and would be their interpreter. Reuben fell into stride beside Joseph as the column circled once round the fort and the big hospital tent which had been set up on the parade ground. Soldiers and treaty Nez Percé in white men's clothes stood around the tent, and from a balcony the wives of officers looked down. Here was a sight to fill the empty pages of their diaries.

All afternoon the braves rode in wild military maneuvers. That night, after pitching their tents outside the compound, they danced. The drums never stopped. But Joseph took no part in any of this. He knew what a Gatling gun looked like, and he knew what it could do. The Nez Percé would not frighten One-Armed Howard with their display, but they would feel better, more sure of themselves perhaps, and that was enough.

The conference began on the third of May, 1877. The Nez Percé, riding into the post, stacked their arms at the gate and then crowded around the tent with its open flaps. They cleared a path as the warriors entered. General Howard was waiting for them behind a camp table. A professor of mathematics turned soldier, he'd lost two horses at Fair Oaks along with his right arm. One thing he had not lost was the thumb-worn Bible he had carried since the Seminole campaign in '57. He had prayed with its help before each battle and major decision in his life. It lay beside him now on the camp table, as formidable as a loaded Colt against the heathen beliefs that surrounded him.

Howard did not rise when the chiefs entered. He did not shake hands, for his right sleeve was pinned up to his shoulder. One by one the warriors shook hands with the other officers, a careful ceremony, the only white ritual they knew well. Joseph offered his left hand to Howard, and the General took it. Their eyes met, forming a momentary bridge. Then both hands and gaze broke away, and Joseph thought, "We are as different as east and west, but somehow I like him." Toohoolhoolzote and Looking Glass did not shake hands with Howard. White Bird did so like a frightened child, and then retired to a corner of the tent.

The council started badly when two old medicine men from the reservation, overcome by the arrival of their wilder kin, began dancing round the tent, shaking their coupsticks. For the first time General Howard stood up, and he said something in English which made the faces of the Indians tighten. The dancing pair quickly vanished, led outside the fort by an escort of soldiers. Then, as if nothing had happened, the one-armed soldier began speaking in altar tones which reminded Joseph of the old days of his baptism when Lapwai was only a mission and not a military outpost. The translation came haltingly to his ears. "You know how I have always respected the Nez Percé, and I have told you before that I thought the old treaty was unfair. I have gone to Washington and have talked long with the Great Chief, and he believes me." The hopeful words came second-hand. Joseph tried to read Howard's face, but it remained a mask, expressionless as the sole of his polished boot. Joseph could not see beyond the eyes. He tried to catch and hold the eyes of the white general for a glimpse of the truth behind the words, but he could not. The words brought him only a vague impression of the great and enormous storm cloud within the white man, which he did not understand and for which he had no name. "In one treaty after another, we have dealt unfairly with our Indian friends. They have not fought us; they have been our friends. Settlers have come, and gold seekers, and sellers of liquor, and your people have accepted them, even when these white men have stolen from your herds. 'What can we do for our friends?' I asked the Great Chief in Washington. 'What can we do to protect and help them?' And he told me, 'We will build them schools.'"

Here Joseph for the first time interrupted. "Tell the Great White Father that we do not want schools."

"Why? They will cost the Indians nothing."

"They will teach us to have churches."

"The churches, too, will be free."

"They will teach us to quarrel about God, as the Catholics and Protestants do at Lapwai. We know God, and we do not quarrel about him."

"Then we will not speak of it here," came the translation. "When I spoke last year with the Great Father and told him how good and kind you had been, I told him he must do something for his Indian children."

And so it went, with Howard speaking as though he had learned it all by heart, the words going round in one orbit, counters in a game of bones to muddle the Nez Percé. Joseph knew that the real talk had not begun, that the words as yet had little to do with their meaning. "I told the Great Father in Washington that we must protect our Indian friends and take them to a safe place free of bad whites. There, each one of you will have a place and land to yourself, and Washington will send tools for you to work the land. Have no fear. You will be well paid for the land where you now live." Then the maps of the proposed reservation were brought out, and they did not contain the Wallowa valley or any of the territory called home by the non-treaty Indians except the corner where Looking Glass had his village. Joseph had expected no better, and made no objection when Howard ended the powwow, saying, "I am tired of speaking. You are tired of listening. I will speak tomorrow." Silently the chiefs, then the soldiers, filed out.

On the following day of council, Toohoolhoolzote rose to speak for the Nez Percé. The dark-corded tendons in his neck stood out and his voice boomed so that his people outside could hear and take heart. "Howard Cut-Off-Arm, you speak always of Washington. Who is this Washington? Is he a white chief, or a lodge, or a place of meeting? Every time you have a powwow, you speak of Washington. Leave Mr. Washington, if he is a chief, alone. He has no sense." Here Toohoolhoolzote, the Dreamer, raised one hand to his mouth with two fingers outstretched and thrust forward. "Washington is two-tongued. He knows nothing about our land. He was never here. And you are always telling us about your cavalry. What do we care of their fighting ability? You are a chief, Howard Cut-Off-Arm, and I am chosen by my people to speak for them. Let us settle the business between us. For a Nez Percé to plow is stupid. Why should we rip up the grass? The earth grows its own grass if it is left alone. When you plow up furrows, you turn the earth into something it did not plan for itself. To plow this way and that is to be as a beast in a cage. And why do you call us your children? We are not your children. We are grown men. We think for ourselves. Washington cannot think for us." Here the Dreamer's voice rose almost to a howl, as though a wolf crouched inside him ready to spring. "The Great Spirit Chief made the world as it is and as he wanted it. He made part of it for us to live upon. I do not see why Washington has the right to move us where he likes."

Through all this, Howard's face had remained as expressionless as a medicine man's mask. He was cool, dispassionate—perhaps, it seemed to Joseph, faintly amused, letting the Indian weary himself with bluster. When Toohoolhoolzote finally folded his arms and stepped back, Howard spoke again tirelessly, ready to begin again from the beginning, unsoftened. It took a man of unusual conviction not to have been persuaded in the slightest degree. But the newspapers had called him an Indian lover because of his fair dealings with the Apaches, and he wanted to set the record straight.

Two more days of council took place. Howard continued to repeat himself, while White Bird spoke hesitantly in behalf of his home, and Looking Glass and Toohoolhoolzote interrupted with veiled threats. There was a weekend postponement during which troops were dispatched to strategic positions. Joseph had not yet spoken when, on the fifth day of council, Howard rose, planting five spread fingers on the table, and spoke plainly. He was very pale and precise. His great black beard gave him the look of a bull buffalo finally brought to bay, but his voice gave away nothing. He had no intention of being crossed. Washington had decided. For their own good, the Indians of the Wallowa must move to the reservation. Sooner or later they would have trouble with the whites, and to avoid this they would have to come in without further delay. They would be well paid, he promised, though no Indian there had seen the wealth promised in the past by Washington. "All right. Does anyone have anything to say?"

The anger that rose in Joseph's heart was an anger he had never known in all his life. Yet from his expression there was no guessing that he was disturbed by Howard's speech. "I will speak tomorrow," he said. Howard made no objection. It would allow more time for the troops to come up.

It seemed a waste of time to talk back and forth, making throat noises, waving one's hands. And yet Joseph had to talk, for it was the last hope, short of war or submission. When he stepped forward to speak on that last day of council, he stood silent and straight for some time. After the long pause, his voice was slow, betraying neither anger nor fear, a manly voice causing all men to listen. It was not as if he were ignoring General Howard, or as if he had failed to hear him, and yet he spoke as one who must say something because the situation demands it. It was as though he talked to himself, for himself, just to hear the words said aloud.

"I have heard in this tent," he began, "that we must sell our land. It would be no different if Washington came to me and said, 'Joseph, I like your horses and I want to buy them.' And I say to him, 'No, my horses suit me, I will not sell them.' Then Washington goes to my neighbor and says, 'Joseph has some good horses. I want to buy them, but he will not sell.' And my neighbor takes the money and says, 'I will sell you Joseph's horses.' Then Washington returns to me and says, 'Joseph, I have bought your horses and you must let me have them.' If we have sold our land to the government, this is the way it was done. A man can sell his horse, a man can have his horse stolen—but a man cannot sell the land where he was born. The Great Spirit, when he made the earth, placed no marks or boundaries upon it. A man is born to the land and grows up on its bosom. It is too sacred to be valued or sold for schools or churches or gold or silver. A man cannot be cut away from the land that bore him."

As he went on, Joseph seemed to grow taller. A warmth radiated from him. He filled the tent. "I wonder, if the ground came to life, what it would say. I hear what this earth says. It says, 'God placed me here.' The earth says that God tells it to take care of the Indians upon the earth. The grass says, 'Feed the horses and cattle.' Everyone is born to part of the earth. It cannot be sold or stolen. God made our bodies from the earth. What shall I do? Shall I give the lands that are part of my body? If your god is all loving, as I have been told, if he is all good and all powerful, why does he let the white man mistreat the Indian? Is he only an echo god used by this Washington?"

At this point Howard, who had sat attentively under his slouch hat, stood up and bared his head. His ears were as red as a mountain sunset and he leaned forward as he must have leaned forward into the cloud of Confederate shot and shell at Fair Oaks and Gettysburg. Then Joseph knew his talk had been for nothing. One could not reason with the white man. He was like a spoiled child without instruction, with no understanding of good or evil.

Howard spoke now with finality. He must be firm but fatherly, so that these Indians would not mistake him as the Seminole had done. It had taken four years to destroy them in the steaming Florida swamps. There would be no more polite rhetoric.

"You . . . have . . . thirty . . . days!" he said, each word the spitting of a bullet. "You must come to the Lapwai Reservation with all your cattle and horses, or they will fall into the hands of white men. Soldiers will protect you. The Army is still good medicine in these parts, and it will enforce the treaty, like it or not. Believe me, the Great White Father may be far away, but his arm is long and his vengeance is total." All this was as abrupt as a tree falling. A long silence followed, impossible to repair entirely. "I'm sorry," he went on, sounding tired, if not indeed sorry. "I have my orders from Washington. Joseph, will you do as you are told?"

"In peace. I can speak only for my people in peace." The tendons in Joseph's cheeks moved. He looked down at the ground. A new watchful realization had come between the two men. They respected one another as before, but now they were enemies.

Looking Glass shouted: "This place is too small for me!" He shouldered his way out. Others followed. The last council was over.

One ritual remained, to examine the reservation land which had been assigned them. Joseph looked with direct and unhurried eyes, but behind them lurked desperation. Howard and two cavalrymen escorted him, together with Looking Glass and White Bird, to select the sites. Toohoolhoolzote had created another disturbance and had been held briefly at the fort, but Howard had agreed to his release and now a surface good nature prevailed. They lunched at a white farm. The owner's name was Caldwell and he was a squatter. Howard promised he would be ousted before the Indians came in. Caldwell stared at his guests as one species of animal will stare at another. Except for Caldwell's rudeness, the day seemed to go as Howard wished.

The territory assigned to Looking Glass was already within the proposed reservation, so his tribe would not have to move. White Bird, eager to avoid trouble, seemed resigned to settle near his old friend. Toohoolhoolzote was unapproachable, speechless with rage and contempt, but his tribe was too small to resist the Army. He would have to take what Howard assigned him or face the consequences. Joseph passed through that long, blind day, seeing the land that would be his, and yet not seeing. He remembered how his father had treated Lawyer's Lapwai treaty, he promising nothing and taking no gifts.

The next day the chiefs left, leading their people home. It was the middle of May. The ice in the lakes and mountains had long since cracked with spring thunder. The frosty bright days of racing clouds had passed over the deep canyons. The time of the frogs' first croaking had brought hail and then rain, and the rivers of the Wallowa had overflowed their banks. How, in thirty days, could Joseph's people move their stock? How could they even think of moving the stock? Once away from the fort, Joseph exhaled slowly, trying to give his nerves time to settle and his brain to clear. There still remained that deep and unreachable unease of a man who lives in a world no longer here, whose world has become a dream. His father's world.

He longed for the wise old man to be back again. How quickly he had become old, as if to escape the darkening wings of the future. Almost overnight his hair had turned white, making him look like an antique replica of himself. Then the flesh had melted from his bones like wax under the heat of some inner flame, and the shaman had come with his pipe and sung his doctoring songs. Death would not be put aside. Old Joseph had been removed from the lodge to the small house of dying. There Young Joseph had gone to him. Perhaps a boy should fear his father, but Joseph never had. He had always loved him, and was a more devoted son on this account than he would ever have been through fear. When Old Joseph spoke in those last hours, the young man took each word to heart. "Let my son speak no English. Keep away from such things." His breath came hard, like the working of a rusty knife in a leather sheath, and his broad face wrinkled into a contortion that was like crying. "My son, when my body returns to the earth and my spirit journeys to the Great Spirit Chief, then you must think of your people. You must close your ears when you are asked to sign a treaty selling your home and this earth that holds your father. Never sell away the bones of your mother or father . . . Joseph, my son, you were born to trouble and sorrow, and it will stay with you all your days . . . Joseph . . . my son . . ." There was a long sigh. His hand slipped lifelessly from his son's grasp.

His father's death had fallen on Joseph like a grinding weight, and yet when the quavering death cry went up and the news ran howling from one lodge to another, Joseph did not cry. It was not a thing to cry over. It was a beautiful thing, this passing—a thing to be gravely considered. In a deep voice he began to chant the song to the darkness and the light beyond.

That night there had been a dance for the dead. A circle of young women leaped on one foot, rocked back, then leaped on the other foot, forcing out their breaths in a harsh "Heh!" Round the heaped fire they kept it up all night until dawn. Then Old Joseph, wrapped in his blankets, with a basket of dried berries and smoked fish beside him, went beneath the ground. Young Joseph shoveled the earth in upon him, and when it was done, he took up a handful of soil and smelled it. The aroma entered him. Home: his valley, his tribe, his family. He loved all three passionately.

Joseph felt that he could give up none of them. Yet to hold out past thirty days meant war, and no matter how he felt about the Bostons, he respected them for their tireless ferocity in war. When the Spokans had fought for their ancestral home, the whites had brought in mountain howitzers and long-range guns, dispersed the braves and hung the leaders. Captain Jack and his Modoc braves had held off the Army for weeks in the California lava beds, but in the end they, too, had been beaten and the leaders hung. The great nation of the Sioux had also fought. They had won for a time, but now they were in exile or on reservations. Even if, years before, all the tribes had united in one war against the whites, even then they would surely have been destroyed.

"What are we to do?" Joseph addressed his brother, who rode beside him.

"It seems to me better to be dead than to be plundered without a fight," said Ollokot.

"We have no chance."

"But we have a choice. The day you ask me to die for my people, I will die."

"I will never ask that of you or any man. I honor my father, but I am not such a man as he."

Nor did he know what his father would do now. Everything had changed so fast since the first chunking paddle-wheelers on the Clearwater had thrown sparks and smoke and cast off wild hooting cries that the bears and deer and Indians stood still and listened to. The

Colonel Wright was the first to come, grounding finally, so that the town of Slaterville had to be built. Next year, with the river lower, another town came about the same way: Lewiston, peopled by banished gamblers and highwaymen and rovers with the gold fever. Like a yeasty ball of dough, the town had spread, down either side of a rutted muddy road. Through its frame buildings the winter wind blew dolefully, for it was an old town already, tired and sagging, its streets a brown slop of mud most of the time and grass growing on what some called sidewalks. And there was the junk and the trash and the debris, over which some Indians squabbled like children. Joseph thought of his own green bottle and how Ollokot now wore its last age-softened fragment around his neck.

When these stealers of Indian land and destroyers of Indian forest had first come to the Wallowa, Joseph had tried to accommodate them. There was room for all at first, and yet he knew that if you gave a white man your finger he'd take the whole arm. From the first, seeds of hatred, fear, and misunderstanding had begun to grow. In those early days Joseph had tried hard. He'd visited the first few settlers. Some stood their ground, viewing him as a mountain lion from the mouth of his cave regards an approaching enemy. Others were willing to talk to him in the Chinook jargon, or even in sign language. A few learned to like him, and he had visited their homes to tell tales of the Wallowa or to talk about his daughter, Spring Song. Sometimes he took along the tall young girl with her smooth moon face and friendly brimming eyes, for he loved her. He loved all children, even the little white ones who had not yet learned suspicion. He remembered now a boy no bigger than a jack rabbit with a worried little face white like a fish's belly. Joseph would have liked to play with that child as his own, to ruffle his hair and to show him the forest. As the boy peered from the door of his cabin, Joseph had slapped his knee for the child to come sit, and he had made a face. Then the child had suddenly given a shriek of pleasure, put his feet together, made three forward jumps, and said "Hello!" Another jump, and the pointing of a finger. "Higgledy-piggledy," the child had remarked emphatically. It meant only that they were friends, exciting friends. But then the mother had intervened. Joseph smiled at her. No harm done. He liked all children, he tried to tell her. But she was apprehensive. The boy was carried off on a pretext, and a thin distressful cry rose from the other room. "Hush," the woman said. "Shhhh. The nasty smelly Indian will give you lice." He knew the word "lice." He sensed her meaning.

Even at best there were such barriers, and the hospitality of a Nez Percé home remained unknown to the settlers. Far worse than the homesteaders were the miners and the rough whiskey sellers who came with them, bringing in whiskey at forty cents a pint, or raw alcohol tinctured with oil of cinnamon. They shortchanged, robbed, murdered the Indians. One of the worst of the whiskey men had been Joe Craig, a drunken bootlegger with an evil eye and a wet mouth, who beat his wife regularly. After getting a Nez Percé drunk in

Lewiston, he had taken him out of town and cut him to pieces. The white judge hadn't even put him before jury. But there had been judgment of a sort. After sampling his own wares to excess, Craig had proceeded to pick his nose with a rusty nail, and died within the week.

Most savage of all the white settlers was Larry Ott, who'd been befriended by Eagle Robe of White Bird's band. When Ott built a fence across Eagle Robe's garden, he'd answered the Indian's protest with a shotgun blast. It was said the dying Eagle Robe had urged his son, Wahlitits, not to avenge his death. Now two years had passed and Larry Ott was still very much alive. So was the farmer Findley, who'd shot down Joseph's cousin, Wilhautyah. Under pressure, the whites had tried Findley for manslaughter and released him.

Twenty-six dead Nez Percé over the years, and not one dead white man. "One day we will arrest a white man," Joseph thought, "and try him. One day. Perhaps!"

Liquor was no good for Indians. Joseph had known that since his first vision quest. Indians never drank to savor the flavor on their tongues or to compare it to other beverages or to enhance food or conversation. They drank to get wild and drunk. Ollokot had never tried it as a boy, but he'd taken a bottle away from an intoxicated brave once and had shown it to Joseph.

"Pour it out, brother. It will do you no good," Joseph had cautioned.

"I had better try it," Ollokot had replied. "I'm a man.

It is right I should find out about these things." So he had thrown back his head and the liquor rippled down slowly, in one long draught. "Ayeee, grandfather. It burns." A pause to consider. "What is it doing to me?"

"It is doing its magic. Do you like it?"

Ollokot belched slowly and regularly. He paused to consider, saying finally: "Everything is good now." Then, fixing Joseph with a fevered eye, he had thrust the bottle neck deep into his gullet and gurgled down the last drop. For a time he talked loudly, drunkenly, with the Great Spirit. Then the heat of the lodge had begun to bother him and he had stood up. He did not weave, but his eyes were slits and his mouth looked ready to slide off his face. "What has it done to me?" he said before running outside. Joseph had followed him after a while and finally found him not ten steps from the lodge, lying in his vomit like a dog.

Liquor was no good for Indians, and drunken Indians were no good for white men, a fact which brought the first settlers and Joseph to their only common cause. Cleaning out the whiskey sellers had been accomplished in one night of brawling when all available whiskey in the valley went into a stream thereafter called Whiskey Creek. It was a brief victory. The settlers soon returned and many of them became entrenched with the dregs and outcasts of white society along the deep gorge of Salmon Creek.

In the last fifteen years the only real Indian threat to the white intruders had been spiritual. It came from a hunchbacked visionary whom the whites said looked like

Daniel Webster. Smohalla was a Wanapum shaman who believed that a savior would come from the east, bringing dead Indians and animals back to life and expelling the whites. This message Smohalla preached from a tule-mat long house on the sandy, windswept banks of the Columbia River, with the aid of songs and dances, to hasten the day of the lost freedom. His Drummer-Dreamer faith had spread to other tribes.

Chief among the Nez Percé believers was Toohoolhoolzote, who had given up all white ways and now wore his hair long, in a roll above his forehead. Joseph could not open his heart to such beliefs, but he loved and feared the old chief despite his blind acceptance. Perhaps he loved him because of it, for Toohoolhoolzote's blindness was more beautiful than the realism of other men. No more could Joseph accept the Jesus religion of the black robes and the cross. No God would hold them if it came to war. To fight the whites would be to die. This could not be, for the earth gave to all people and creatures but one gift-life—and it was up to each one to use it well.

It had taken Joseph a week of soul-searching to reach his decision. The women were already out digging into the slopes with sharp sticks for kouse roots, which they would boil down into meal. The younger girls were gathering berries and wild onions in the valleys. Strawberries and serviceberries would come later on the upper slopes, but by then there would be no one left to pick them in the Wallowa. He would prepare his own family first. Outside the lodge, the old dog seemed to grin in happy welcome. He had gotten into trouble with a porcupine, and Joseph could only push the needles through his lips and pull them out from inside. There was still swelling, but no infection.

Joseph lowered himself into the lodge with the dog at his heels. For winter, it was dug deep into the ground and thatched over, with a fireplace in the center. Long thin slices of venison hung on the drying and curing rack in the slow heat. He saw the tanned robes hung along the walls and the buckskin lovingly folded. The old squaw's sewing basket held a coil of dry sinew. She had never taken to the white man's thread. His daughter, Spring Song, was there. He watched the lithe way she stirred the great clay pot on the fire. With long legs, narrow hips, and square thin shoulders, she was not built for mothering, he thought, but she was fine in motion . . . a deer . . . And she listened with her head cocked to one side as he began to tell her softly what must be done. She was young, and could take such news better. It was easier, beginning with her. But when he had finished, she was looking at her hands in her lap. She had not said a word in return.

"I'm sorry," he told her. "There is no other way. Now I must tell the others."

She rose and looked at him. There were tears in her eyes.

"A princess never cries," he said softly.

"Poor Father. What hurts each one of us hurts you." She touched his cheek with her hand, the mere brushing of a bird's wing. To reassure him? To reassure herself? He did not know, but he felt the tears behind his eyes and forced them back. "Your hand is warm," he said. "I must tell your mother now." Spring Song went to the entry. She did not look back, and in one smooth, silent motion she passed from the lodge.

"She isn't a deer," he thought. "She is a butterfly . . . or a swallow." He should mind not having sons, but he did not. His young wife, Singing Beads, was the same sort, too slim for easy mothering, but wanting more children than the one she had. Now she was due any day for the second time, and he must tell her that her child would be born on the trail.

Joseph knelt beside her where she slept, all wrapped in trade blankets. Her slow breath smelled of milk, sweet and strange. Tenderness was not part of him, but ever since the day she had left him speechless and stunned by laughing in his face when she should have hung her head, he had loved her without reservation. When she sang for him in a low pure voice, his soul was lifted, and he had taught her songs she had no business knowing, warriors' songs, because of those special qualities he knew in her.

"Palojami," he said, "fair one, we must talk."

Her walnut-brown eyes came open, knowing, unsurprised, and then she smiled. Those eyes were so good to live in that he had never, since first seeing them, known where else to go.

"We must talk," he said.

Her eyes were wide now, flirtatious.

"You are shameless," he said. "To make such eyes. Look at you, round as the earth. Now listen."

"My ears are listening. It is good to talk with my husband." She put a cool hand on the back of his neck.

"Hear me. This is not just talk." He could not be really stern with her, and yet she pretended to pout. "Don't be angry."

"I'm not angry."

"Smile then," he commanded, and she would not lift her face until he put his finger under her chin. "Smile." In the end he told her all, and then she, too, was somber. Her eyes changed to so sad a darkness, so gentle and so grave, that they killed in him all sensation except protective love.

"You will see your family," he told her. "Your father, Whisk-Tasket, spoke of you when I was at Lapwai."

"I have forgotten that life," she said. It was many winters now since Joseph had taken his bride from among the treaty Nez Percé. "Do you care for me?" Singing Beads asked finally, serious now, needing reassurance.

"Like the light of my eyes," he replied.

"Then all will be well. I'm not afraid."

He had then to inform his first wife, Strikes Standing. He did not love that one, but there was no woman for whom he had greater respect. She was thick with work, though she had borne him no children. Strikes Standing did common things uncommonly well, and she had great gifts: for finding honey and herbs, for feeling a storm long before the sky darkened. She could warble and reply to the notes of different birds, and often she would whistle and sing their tunes for pure joy of spirit.

Joseph found her outside, rubbing the brains of a slain deer into its stretched hide to soften it. She smelled of burned-out fires, rawhide, and sweat, and he talked to her like a man.

"Harken, squaw of wind and trouble."

She knew without being told. She went on with her work, her mouth closed. They'd discussed it before, yet now something final had happened.

"Shall I load the travois?" she asked finally.

"First I must tell the old woman and the others. But be ready."

His own mother had died when he was small. The old woman he spoke of was his father's woman. She was in his charge now, and though she was not his blood, he was fond of her. Tiny, inconspicuous, she was sunning on a rock like a lizard.

"How are you, Grandmother?" he asked.

"I was thinking of your father," she said.

The old woman's face was brown and crisscrossed, her cheeks crevassed from sun and wind, laughter and tears. Lightning-like wrinkles across her forehead came from hunger, and labor, and fear of war. All this he could read in the face of the aged woman, but her hair remained a wonder. Silky and fine as a moth's cocoon, it was the longest and strangest he had ever seen. All her beauty was in her hair.

When he told her, she took his wrist tightly in her small dry hand. She did not cry, but there was a sound from her lips as though something inside her was being torn. He tried to tell her she would be better off at Lapwai, more comfortable, but he knew that she would not go. Perhaps it was well. She was so bent forward now with age and former burdens that she came close to walking on all fours. Even if she survived the journey, she would not live long on the reservation. Better to die in her home; better perhaps for them all.

He had already talked with Ollokot, who, at least on the surface, had accepted Joseph's decision. So it remained only to speak to the warriors. This he did that afternoon. They could go peacefully to Lapwai with their cattle and horses, they could wait for the white soldiers to herd them in, or they could fight. In no way could they win, so it was best, he told them, to go in peace. The days in freedom were over. He made the sign for an end, forever. The old songs had been sung. The old ways were gone.

The following day the women packed and the men drove in what stock they could find. At dawn they would move, but when a trace of day came into the sky they stood reluctant to make the first move. They were afraid. The hills took shape against the light and then the mountains became visible. The campfires paled until they no longer threw a circle of light. The stars vanished. Still the people hesitated, seeing the dawn, their hills and canyons, their Wallowa for the last time.

"How can there be an end?" Ollokot said. "There is a roundness to everything. The day, the earth." He made the sign of the circle, the never ending.

"But yesterday is gone," Joseph replied. "The day before that is gone. They will not return. I will give the signal. It is time we move."

"Perhaps it is already too late," Ollokot mused.

But they moved off together, Joseph's people. He was a father to them. For men twice his age he was a father in the old tribal way, and they trusted him and followed without question. On the hills behind, they could see horsemen, white riders, come to brand the ponies the braves had not had time to catch. The whites were always branding the Indian stock because they knew the Indians had no friends who would plead their cause before the law councils.

As Joseph had expected, the old woman stayed behind. He left her in a small lodge with blankets, dried meat, and meal cakes. They would last for a time and then, if the bears or the white men did not finish her first, she would die, which was what she wanted. It was not his right to obstruct an old person's wish. It was not the Indian way.

They made good time the first days, moving down the steep grassy divide to the banks of the Snake River. From a distance the river looked asleep, flat. Then a swirled log would roll by, and the powerful and warning whisper of it grew like a herd of distant buffalo running fast. "It's a strong dark god," Joseph thought, "hungry and vengeful in the springtime. It will gobble some of us up."

A few of the younger braves rode their ponies into the river, daring it to pull them down. These few struggled across. For the rest, bullboats were made of buffalo robes and pine frames. Into these went the old, the young, and the baggage. Four ponies were tied to each and driven into the stream. The riderless animals were made to swim on their own, and many were swept away. A few of the bullboats, along with their baggage, also were lost, but no human lives.

Finally only Joseph and Ollokot remained to cross. They sat their ponies on the near bank and Joseph thanked the river for its humanity in sparing his women and his tribe.

"I hope we are doing the right thing, grandfather," Ollokot said before plunging into the stream.

"No," Joseph replied. "But it is the only way."

Then the icy current took them and they fought for the far shore. Nothing then was left on the Wallowa side except the old dog, who ran back and forth. He raised a forlorn howl and finally followed. He was a poor swimmer, moving with rapid jerks, his head held high. When he arrived at the far bank, he was too tired to climb out. Joseph had to help him up. The dog tried to lick his face, staggered, tried to shake himself, and nearly fell. But they were across, all of them.

III
First Blood

Since time immemorial, the Nez Percé had met at Teaphlewam on the southern fringe of the Camas Prairie beside Lake Tolo. Although the Salmon River was at flood, Joseph's band crossed without loss of life, though some of their stock drowned and more remained on the far bank. On the second day of June, 1877, they met for the last time in freedom with Toohoolhoolzote and White Bird and their people.

There was an air of desperate festivity about the occasion. A dangerous gaiety infected the young braves, who strutted about like turkey gobblers. "One-Armed Howard has shown us the rifle!" they shouted. Toohoolhoolzote encouraged the unrest. He had been dishonored by the white men, who had thrown him into prison. Only blood could wash away the disgrace. In a fight, he told them, the old gods would return in their strength to help the Nez Percé. Old ways would return. The other chiefs saw no good in such talk, but they consented to a parade through camp in the hope that it would lead to horse racing.

Wahlitits rode at the end of the column with Red Moccasin Tops, whose reputation was bad. After the procession, the braves raced and played the bone game. They talked of unpunished murders and the recent imprisonment of Toohoolhoolzote, and discharged their guns into the dusk.

"They sing for blood," Looking Glass said. "It is a good song."

"It is a dangerous song," Joseph replied.

"With you, my brother, and White Bird, I would fight the troopers gladly. But I do not want to be surprised into war by foolish braves, or by that old Dreamer, Toohoolhoolzote."

"See his eyes," said Joseph, "how they glitter in the firelight."

"Watch him carefully. I am going home," Looking Glass replied. And, though it was early evening, he rounded up his braves and set out for his camp on the reservation.

With the dark, great fires sprang up and dancing began. The warriors shouted and sang, all bone and muscle and wild joy, leaping round the flames and through them, as natural and untamed as the mountain waterfalls. Louder and louder they kept on, with the drums running through the song like the compounded heartbeat of the performers. Sparks from the fires, sparks from the warriors, flew upward, threatening a world that was denied them.

Two weeks remained until Howard's deadline for them to be at the reservation, but Joseph was for pressing on in the morning. White Bird disagreed. "Your father came to this place in summer, and his father. I am an old man with few winters remaining. I will taste of the good fish in the streams and sing the old songs in freedom for the last time."

Joseph replied: "I tell you, grandfather, the old days are gone. There is an end to them."

He might have had his way, were it not for Toohoolhoolzote, who said: "Then we will smoke our pipes and dream. We will dream the old days as they were." Thus the old chiefs stood together, and Joseph's respect for them was great.

"Grandson," White Bird said, "the salmon are running in the river. Think how many we can catch with the nets. And there will be time to butcher and smoke the stock which could not cross the river." So Joseph submitted to older, if not wiser, counsel. He did, however, speak to Ollokot, who returned empty-handed from the bone game.

"You were foolish," Joseph told him. "You are no good at gambling. Did you lose your ponies?"

Ollokot grinned sheepishly. "What else could I have done? It was fine play. I was happy."

Then Joseph told him of his fears. Ollokot shrugged them off. There was some liquor in White Bird's band, and a few troublemakers, but not many. None but a few hotheaded braves spoke of war.

"And Toohoolhoolzote the Dreamer," Joseph said.

"That one is too old to lead warriors. He can only mutter."

"Are his braves without ears?"

Nothing happened that night or the next day. The braves exhausted themselves with fishing by day and dancing and gambling at night. On the morning of the third day at Teaphlewam, the wind was high. Joseph rose with the sun, planning to recross the Salmon River and retrieve some of the abandoned herd. The calm of exhaustion lay over the camp. He surveyed the sky. Like cracks in spring ice, the cloud ceiling had begun to break and lift away toward the mountain peaks. It would be a good day, Joseph observed, as he rode toward the Salmon River with the wind behind him. His heart seemed lighter than it had been. Ollokot rode at his side. They raced their horses, and it was good to command all those ripples of sinew and muscle. Side by side they crossed the river, which was cold and bracing. That, too, was good.

During the morning, other braves crossed over to help round up the stray cattle. Those that seemed strong enough were driven across the Salmon and on to the camp. The rest had to be butchered, and the meat, which Joseph had always found too sweet, smoked with all possible speed. The butchery went on all afternoon. Joseph was sickened by it. But one did not waste food. A massive carving and separating followed by the light of crackling fires, and when the fires were low and smoldering, the smoking process began. It would go on the better part of a week. The meat was stringy and tough, with the juice and fat drained out by the winter.

It was near the end of the second week in June when they recrossed the river. The weather was bright and blustery. Ollokot and Joseph rode ahead of the twelve-pack animals. Joseph felt apprehensive. He wasn't sure why. Singing Beads was in Strikes Standing's capable hands. The cool mountain air whipped their hair and their horses' manes. Inevitably, the brothers raced, not to win or lose, but for the pure joy of motion. Joseph's horse seemed more to flow than to gallop, yet he heard the light thud of hoofs on the packed plain and felt the sliding flank muscles beneath him. His blood sang. Swift as thought they were, and that wild ripple of life while it lasted seemed to carry him into another world. Above the camp the brothers halted, both winners, hugging their ribs and laughing with the pleasure of being alive.

Then something about the camp, though still far away, caught their attention. Joseph felt a stirring among the roots of his hair. The wind carried the sound to them intermittently, a quick repetition of beats, then a stumbling stroke. They looked at one another. War drums; a slow and steady pulse which grew louder as they rode forward.

Throughout the camp there was an air of impatience and hatred. Joseph could hear it in the mutter of the drums, in the boisterous chanting of the braves proclaiming their devotion to old gods. Bands of warriors rode back and forth, brandishing rawhide shields and bows. Their bodies were painted for war: red streaks down the center of the hair, orange on the forehead for strength, dotted lines in yellow, green, black over cheeks and eyelids and body for their guardian Wyakins. A few wore wolves' heads and buffalo heads. Their horses, too, were decorated for battle, with zigzag stripes of color.

Squaws snatched children out of their way. Dogs yipped, horses reared, and the braves shouted to one another of deeds of valor not yet performed.

Joseph was approaching his own lodge when Wahlitits, of White Bird's band, rode up like the war god of a song. He reined in his mount; the horse gave a low whistling cry and completed a dozen arching steps, coming down hard on its forelegs each time. Just to look at Wahlitits told Joseph that something fearful and unchangeable had happened, even before the brave held high a tomahawk, its dark blade crusted with blood and hair.

"What have you done?" Joseph demanded. "Tell me, so that I will know what to do."

Wahlitits looked at him long, with opaque eyes—the ruthless eyes of a killer brimful of hate. "I have avenged my father," he said. "Blood for blood." His teeth and eyes glittered, and he rode off without another word. Joseph looked grimly about. The camp was in panic. Tipis were being struck, travois loaded.

Finally it was Two Moons, the wise old warrior with a touch of autumn gold in his eyes, who told the tale second-hand. "They have killed the white man," he said.

"Who? Who has done this killing?"

"The one you just saw. Red Moccasin Tops. And Swan Necklace."

"Swan Necklace? He's only a boy." He was sixteen and, like the others, from White Bird's people.

Joseph's face remained inscrutable, but the news struck him like the edge of a tomahawk wielded by a giant. Two Moons's voice flowed like a stream of gurgling water. The pictures evoked by the old man's words were clearer than the words themselves. It was two days past. Wahlitits had ridden his horse through the drying kouse roots spread before the lodge of one Yellow Grizzly Bear. Enraged, but no match for the young brave in fight, fair or foul, Yellow Grizzly Bear had shouted: "If you are so brave, why don't you kill the white man who killed your father?"

At this Wahlitits had stopped. Then he had wheeled around, seeming about to ride over his heckler. "You will be sorry for your words, grandfather!" he had shouted. That night, while the braves were dancing, he had approached his old friend, Red Moccasin Tops, and his young nephew, Swan Necklace. He had filled their minds with whiskey fumes and visions of honor and revenge. He had stuffed their hair full of eagle feathers, and in the darkness they had ridden off down White Bird Hill to the Salmon River gorge where Larry Ott and their other white tormentors lived.

They could not cross the river to Ott's cabin—it was too wide and rapid—but no light showed and no ribbon of smoke blew from the chimney, so they assured themselves that Ott was not at home and continued down the river. Their blood was up and one white man's death was as good as any other.

A mile farther on lived old Richard Devine. Hadn't he set dogs on them once? And hadn't he killed poor crippled Dakoopin, a Nez Percé with a withered leg? Shot him down when Dakoopin was barely able to drag himself away, let alone defend himself? Dawn was in the treetops when they arrived, but they took time to braid red flannel in their hair. They helped each other with war paint. This was a moment to savor.

The pictures were so vivid in Joseph's mind that he could almost believe he had seen it with his own eyes: the sun rising, the smoking cabin, the three braves stealing forward as though it were a dangerous foe and not a drunken old recluse who awaited them, unknowing. There was no sound but their own breathing. No twig snapped. No dog barked. And then from behind the sod-caulked logs of that windowless cabin rose a moist, groaning voice in song. Did he know? Had he seen them? Even now, was he looking at them down the beaded sight of a cocked buffalo rifle? For a time they froze, waiting. When the singing died on a thick cough, they were suddenly in motion again, knives and tomahawks drawn. The door banged open on screaming hinges.

Richard Devine awaited them, an almost empty whiskey bottle in one hand and his chin settled on his chest. He stared crookedly up from under shaggy brows. Seeing them, his first expression seemed that of disappointment. He had longed for a friend. Seeing the blades, he stood up. He was all unbuttoned down the front. Heavy gray underwear showed through. It was said he changed it four times a year, once for every season. Suddenly the haze before his eyes must have cleared, and in that instant he knew. He saw his death, for a look of naked terror filled his face. The worm had turned. His gun stood in the corner. Too late for that, but he leapt away and clawed at the thick logged wall as though he might break through to safety.

They heard his exclamation, a sharp indrawn shout. He scuttled toward the corner where the gun had stood, but the gun was gone. Several times they circled the room without a blow being struck; three with knives and hatchets, one with a broken bottle held by the neck, all of them moving in dreamy slow motion. Wahlitits lunged first with his hatchet and missed. Devine was quick for an old man. His whiskey bottle left a ribbon of blood along the brave's right arm, but again the hatchet struck. A brown and knotted sinew of an arm lifted the weapon and brought it down, "Hah," with a furious explosion of breath. Devine stood for a moment as if holding his breath, then his knees crumpled. His body slid to the floor. The broken bottle rolled away. Again and again Wahlitits brought down the splintering hatchet. Long cords and bubbles of blood splashed the floor. Bits of scalp and white hair clung to the blade, but Devine would not die. He gave off heavy animal pants, loud and quick. His glassy eyes protruded. He did not know that he lived, but his body clung to life. Wahlitits planted his hand against that face and one round eye stared from between his fingers. Again the blade thudded down. The others helped with their knives, rip-rip-rip.

Finally, blood-smeared and panting, they backed off with their weapons. They had done it. They had really done it. The three of them were shocked and proud and grinning like totems. Wahlitits leaned against the cabin wall, waiting for his breathing to ease and his heart to slow.

It might have stopped there, a life for a life. They could have bundled the corpse into the stream, and no one would have known or much cared. Then they found Devine's whiskey. After that, only exhaustion or death could have stopped them. Before the day was done, three more white men lay dead. But they touched no women. Henry Elfers, who had held a gun on Indians while his partner beat them with an iron cinch ring, was next. They took Elfers by surprise, shot him with his own gun, then took it along with his roan racing stallion. Two other Indian haters, Robert Bland and Henry Beckroge, were caught in the fields and cut down. A whiskey-selling store owner, Samuel Benedict, who had regularly shortchanged them and once had killed a drunken Nez Percé, got away with a wounded leg. By then the liquor was running out, along with their blood lust, so they rode back to camp, with Swan Necklace galloping ahead on Elfers's roan stallion to spread the news.

Not until the following morning, June 15, had Joseph returned to hear the story. Two Moons had told it to the end and now he made the cut-off sign. The story was finished. Finished, Joseph thought, like the stone that falls into the still lake. The stone vanishes, but the ripples . . . how far they travel. Yet there was one hope, and one only. The murderers all came from White Bird's band. His own people were free of blame. Perhaps he could stop the ripples there. He would call a council.

First he made the mistake of returning to his lodge, though it did not seem a mistake at the time. Strikes Standing greeted him there, cool, flat-footed. The din of the camp, not even a tornado could tear such a woman from her feet. Her eyes were half smiling, her voice matter-of-fact.

"You have a child," she said.

"Thank you, grandmother."

Singing Beads lay inside. She looked dead, her face a small ashen mask. "Are you well?" he asked. She nodded, trying to smile. "Is it a man child?"

"A girl," she said. She indicated the child, asleep and already strapped to a cradle board. "Whatever we are, we are yours."

Joseph took up the infant in his hands. She looked like a freshly skinned jack rabbit. He saw the little dark red face and the curled hands, and his chest seemed too small for his heart. "It is well," he said. Since twice, before the child was born, he had dreamed of a milk-white horse with its colt lying in the snow, he added, "We will call her Snow Pony." Strange, this happiness—an island of it, while disaster raged round about. At the same time Wahlitits had raised his tomahawk, Strikes Standing must have taken the knife to cut this life from its mother's body. New life and death, all by violence.

He had not intended at first to worry Singing Beads about the happenings outside, but she had overheard the tumult. As was always the case between these two, he could withhold nothing in the end. The news made her chin tremble. She must have wanted to cry, but she was the daughter of a chief, and the wife of one.

"It isn't war yet," he told her. "There will be a council. I won't let my daughter be born into war."

The council met within the hour. Toohoolhoolzote urged war. White Bird remained silent. Joseph insisted strongly that war was hopeless. He spoke of the whites, of their numbers and their weapons, of how they fought not to show bravery but to kill. "The only hope for us," he said, "is not to draw the tomahawk; to hold still and speak with the white man."

"The tomahawk is already red with blood," White Bird reminded him. "We must leave this land."

Outside in the camp the tumult grew. Drums filled the air with muffled beats. The wind whipped the lodge flaps.

"Reddened with blood by your braves, White Bird, not mine," Joseph replied. "Three of your people have done bad things. They must be turned over." Against this suggestion there was general protest. "It is not my wish. It is what must be done, grandfather, or we all will be at war. When the war is lost, they will hang the chiefs that made it. They will put a rope around your neck, grandfather, and choke off your spirit so that it may never rise. Your spirit will lie buried forever with your body." Joseph said this, not because he believed it, but because he knew that White Bird did. "I will not have this death. I will not have my braves killed because you cannot control your braves, grandfather. I will take them to Lapwai and leave you to fight One-Armed Howard."

"I will flee to the Land of the Old Queen," said White Bird, although he knew the Canadian border was hundreds of miles to the north.

"The click-clack will send their messages and the troopers will catch you. You will hang by the neck, grandfather, and your people will be scattered."

Outside, the chanting of the braves rose in the distance like the hum of angry bees streaming from a hive, spoiling for a fight.

Inside the lodge, the fight was over. White Bird had given in. Toohoolhoolzote was old; he could not fight alone. So they prepared the pipe in agreement. Joseph smoked first, chanting: "O Sun, O you above people, pity us and help us." Then he blew smoke toward the floor. "O Earth Mother, pity us and help us." He passed the pipe on to White Bird, and so it moved among them. When all had smoked, the pipe returned to Joseph, and he knocked the ashes out upon the ground. Then the men rose to go and tell their people what had been decided.

They emerged into a dazzle of sunlight, the quick beat of a tom-tom, and the hurrying thunder of horses' feet. A woman cried out: "Aye . . . ayee!" as the war party flew past. Joseph flung himself after the last pony, was hurled aside. He cast about for a mount, but only plodding pack animals stood near.

"Whose braves are those?" he demanded.

"They are of my band," White Bird admitted. "They are young and rebellious. They do not hear the old men." As he spoke, White Bird seemed the shrunken distillation of all old men, and for a moment Joseph wanted to assure him that all would be well. It wasn't so. But for his own tribe there was still hope. As yet, not one of his braves had spilled blood. He and Ollokot spoke to them calmly. They seemed to listen quietly enough, and during the solemn words of the brothers bound their furies. Not until midnight, full of liquor, derring-do, and the prophetic urgings of Toohoolhoolzote, did a handful of the younger braves slip away from camp to meet in the open prairie, where they pledged to settle matters with the white man Norton, a homesteader on Cottonwood Creek.

Rumors of murder and pillage began arriving at the Nez Percé camp next morning even before Joseph knew his braves were gone. Ollokot brought in the news, and it was like an arrow planted in Joseph's heart. For a long time he sat with his head cupped in his hands. He found himself trembling all over like a stampeded pony. Faintly he heard the war drums, low and steady. There was no more holding back. There was blood on his people's hands now—on his hands. He could not desert them, even for his family's sake. They must be led until the end. Joseph stood erect, squared his shoulders, gathered his resolution, and strode through camp.

"Go. Strike the tipis!" he shouted. "Strike the tipis! The next sun must not find us here."

IV
In White Bird Canyon

Before the Nez Percé broke camp entirely, scouts spread down the different trails. The first reports they brought back were generally untrue. Some said that the whites were in flight all over the territory, others that the Army was converging in four columns to kill them all to the last child. A few Nez Percé rode into the town of Mount Idaho and tried to buy powder and ammunition. They offered two silver dollars for half a can of powder, and were refused. There some treaty Nez Percé described to them how the rampaging braves had cut the tongues out of little girls and killed a boy by crushing his head between the knees of a powerful warrior. These stories weren't true, either. It was fighting men the Nez Percé were after, and the truth was fatal enough: between White Bird Canyon and Slate Creek, and up and down the Salmon River, fifteen white settlers had been killed. Throughout the territory, fearful homesteaders spread tales of horror and alarm that came back to Joseph and his people.

Joseph felt a strange relief, a lifting of doubt. No choice remained now, and there was pride, somehow, in striking back after years of forbearance, in making war against a power ten times as strong. Perhaps they might succeed where other tribes had failed. But Joseph knew this could not happen. Pure courage and love of home could not stand against the martialing of armies, against the rapid-firing guns and cannon, and the singing wire with which the white man instantly called his legions from beyond the hills. And yet the hope still burned. One could not live without hope.

Even among the Nez Percé, there was dissension. Looking Glass, who had come out with some of his people to join in the racing—Looking Glass, who always shouted war in the councils—now washed his hands of them. His people had no blood on their hands. He wanted nothing of these murders, and he turned back south toward the Kamiah Reservation. With Fort Lapwai and its garrison to the northwest, and more cavalry reported coming in from the west, the best hope seemed to be southeast in White Bird Canyon. The place had been named for Chief White Bird and it was where he and his people had a winter home.

Joseph gave the order to move out. White Bird, sunk in gloom at the anticipation of being hung, rode beside him. Ollokot brought up the rear of the slow column of travois-pulling pack animals, wandering stock, squaws, and children. Singing Beads refused to lie in a travois, but she consented to ride, since she was the wife of a chief. Strikes Standing bore the new baby on her back. So they traveled steadily and silently until dusk. On the following morning they crossed the Camas Meadows, so lush and fully green it was hard to keep the ponies from wandering. Finally the trail led steeply down into the wide gorge of the Salmon River. White Bird Canyon was cut by ancient streams into many ridges. About two miles from the river, they camped on a small plateau.

Apart from a rocky backbone jutting up like the spine of some half-buried dinosaur, and two small grassy knolls, this spot was devoid of features. On two sides, the descending banks were eroded and steep. Joseph felt that here they could not be taken by surprise, and he rode over every foot of ground with Ollokot and White Bird. White Bird muttered about retreat, but Joseph said: "If we must fight, we will fight here."

None of them wanted that. White Bird was overcome with fear of the hangman. He dreamed of his strangled son, and continued to favor flight—endless flight, across the border to the Land of the Old Lady, where Sitting Bull already brooded in exile. Joseph had other plans. Perhaps the offending braves, most of whom had rejoined their tribes, could still be turned over to white justice, though it seldom meant justice for Indians. One had only to ask those already hung. But it remained a possibility, if Joseph could arrange a conference before there was a pitched battle. At least the guilty braves could be driven into the hills to fend for themselves. He would even surrender himself as a token, to suffer white vengeance. He would do it gladly, if his death would pay for the past.

Behind all his planning lay the likelihood of war. Most of the braves thought they were at war already. He could see it in the way they grinned as they caught his eye, all nervous and warm and united as people always are in the excitement of facing a common danger. So with Ollokot he laid plans for this last possibility.

"Toohoolhoolzote says we will have a great victory,"

Ollokot said. "He is a Dreamer, and the braves listen. He has made a war song."

"War sings loud enough without his voice," Joseph replied. "Now hear me. We have less than a hundred braves."

"Some are drunk," Ollokot said.

"They will sober up, and most of them have guns."

"Some have repeaters," said Ollokot, who himself carried a brass-framed Winchester with a charm of weasel skin and raven feathers tied to the trigger guard to guide each shot. There were also a few repeating Henry rifles, some plains rifles, and a motley collection of flint and percussion trade arms made by Leman and Barnett when the beaver trade was still good. Joseph seldom carried a gun. He relied on his Wyakin, his own spirit magic, and he knew now without doubt how the whites would come when they came. They would follow the Indian trail down the gorge and onto the plateau. Near the two small knolls he would receive them in parley, and if that failed . . . He drew on the ground with a stick. "Here and here" the braves would wait until the talk was done and, if it came to a fight, Ollokot would lead them out on their ponies.

Ollokot was the perfect battle leader simply because he could not imagine being killed. The Happy Hunting Ground might have suited him, but he did not believe in it. He could not picture oblivion. He could only picture himself living, riding an unbroken pony with the wind in his face, fishing the deep and roaring streams for salmon, firing an arrow into the sun for the sheer joy of its sunlit flight. Joseph knew all this about his brother and was afraid for him.

"There must be no scalping," Joseph told him. "Let us fight with honorable weapons if we must fight."

Ollokot agreed to this. He had never scalped a man, and never would; it was not the Nez Percé way. Even the drunken raiders who had killed the whites had not done that. They had killed only Indian haters, or so they said, to settle old scores. When Patrick Price had come from the shelter of his cabin to save a little girl and had opened his shirt front, telling them to shoot him if they had to kill someone, those red-eyed killers had been touched. They had told him to go with the child in peace.

For the Nez Percé chiefs, the day of planning passed. Then came the day of waiting, and the long night. Joseph lay awake in the stillness before dawn when the dew was forming. He hugged his robe about him, a protection and a comfort against the coming day. At night he led no one. He was alone and confused. "I am a coward," he thought. "Not for my body, but for my people." He did not want their blood on his hands, but if it came to fighting, he would urge them on. If he did not, they would fight anyway, but if he led them, they would rejoice. Either way, it must end badly.

The sun was scarcely above the canyon rim when a sentinel, Seeskoomkee, galloped into camp. Joseph received him and the report spread. Braves prepared their medicine packs wherein lay their strength. Softly they sang songs derived from the spirit powers as they stripped to their clouts. Finally they decorated their bodies with war paint, especially red, the rainbow color for protection.

More sentinels, imitating the quavering cry of the coyote, told of the cavalry's approach down the long grassy draw toward the two buttes where the warriors waited. Joseph watched from the hillside through the white man's magic tube. Ten times on the fingers of both hands he counted the troopers. In the advance party, he recognized Lieutenant Thaller, whom he knew from Lapwai. A good man, Thaller. Behind were civilians. They looked tired and saddle-weary. Probably they had ridden all night, and now it was morning and growing hot.

As the troopers approached in columns of twos, squaws drove in the stock, separating the best spare mounts for their men in case of a fight. At Joseph's signal, Vicious Weasel led out the Nez Percé delegation. There were six of them, bearing a white flag. "Thaller looks tired, but I think he will talk," mused Joseph. "It's the volunteers I don't trust." He recognized Ad Chapman in his big white sombrero. He was an Indian hater with a temper like a gray wolf, always ready to spring.

From the hillside, all appeared remote and calm. The two advance parties closed at a walk; the troopers and braves held back. Surely, Joseph thought, the whites wanted battle no more than he. Surely their mouths went dry at the thought of slaughter, and shivers of fear went through them at the image of broken limbs and heads, at the thought of all the pain. The figures were now one hundred yards apart. Then, as Joseph watched through the glass, he saw Ad Chapman raise his rifle, saw the tiny puff of smoke long before he heard the report. An Indian fired back, and a young trumpeter rolled from his saddle and lay still.

The impossible thing, the thing no one wanted, was happening. Rifles crackled as the six Indians turned back at a gallop. Joseph heard the war drums low and steady from the camp, crying death to the white men. They came for war, then let them have war. The lance which had stood upright in his hand now dipped forward, and the braves, who had been leaning limply over the bone pommels of their rawhide saddles, gave a shrill hackle-lifting yell. As one, their horses lunged forward, sweeping onto the plain with manes and tails flowing.

The cavalry dismounted to receive them: soldiers in the center, the civilian volunteers taking a rocky knoll to the left. Two Moons led out his sixteen warriors in a long curve. He headed straight for the volunteers, while Ollokot, with Wahlitits and Sarpsis Illppilp, emerged from the right and charged Trimble's mounted troops. Their red blankets were good targets, deliberately flaunting their bravery. Ad Chapman was the first to turn tail. Running with great jack-rabbit leaps, he fled with his coat billowing and his rifle cast away. The other civilians ran after him like blind men, falling, running again, bumping into one another. Lieutenant Thaller, his flank exposed, made a stand with eighteen soldiers. There was a rock wall at their backs, and they died where they stood, like brave men.

With no bugler to give signals, confusion reigned among the troopers. A second charge on fresh ponies, with the warriors reloading and firing at full gallop, broke the last resistance. Panic-ridden and for the most part weaponless, the troopers fled after the settlers, back up the canyon in the direction of Mount Idaho. At 6:30 A.M. by the white man's reckoning, it was over. Three Indians had been slightly wounded, one seriously, but over thirty whites lay dead upon the field, along with sixty-three rifles and a few pistols.

After a brief pursuit, Ollokot rode up to his brother. "Grandfather, we have won!" he shouted, and Joseph threw his arms around him. He felt fierce pride. There comes a time when men do what they must, for their home and for their people, when they are willing to die if there is no other way. His heart was bursting with love for his brother and for all his people. They were his one concern. Not the Great Spirit, not himself, only the people, and for them this was a great day. It was only later, walking over the battlefield where the corpses lay, that he saw beyond the horizon, seemed to hear the whine of the singing wire spreading the news. It was the Indian way to live in the day alone, though Joseph knew it was the days to come that mattered. With joyless perseverance, the white man would already be planning the revenge to come. War and fighting were simple answers. All day the camp would be in a delirium of celebration, but these were Indian answers, wrong ones when it came to fighting the white man. Yet Joseph could not help rejoicing in that one day. Whatever the future held, it was truly a great thing that had happened in White Bird Canyon.

When Joseph returned to his tipi, all his women were there. Filled with hope and uncertainty, they waited for his words. "This day is beautiful," he said, "and so is this small one." He held the baby aloft close to the pine ridgepoles where the tipi opened to the sky. "Look, how unafraid she is," he said, "what big eyes. She sees everything."

The sunset glowed in Singing Bead's cheeks. She bit her lips as if with vexation, but she said nothing. It was Strikes Standing who spoke. "Should I pack the travois?" she asked him.

"We have no need for that now. Have you no ears?"

Outside there was gleeful shouting: "Ai-yah! Ai-yah!" Victory! The tom-tom beat round and huge, the very pulse of Mother Earth.

"You will eat army rations today," he said. "Salt beef and biscuits." Then, in a kind of contradiction, to his twelve-year-old daughter, Spring Song: "But when we move, little sister, you must help your mother. You are almost grown."

"There will be more war?" she asked.

"What do you know of war?"

"I think it means we have to die."

"Die? Not a brave was killed today. Hear them."

He smiled a false smile. So much effort went into postponing unhappiness. No one questioned him, though. Singing Beads seemed to plead with her eyes, asking him to say what was in his heart.

"Will there be more fighting?" Spring Song persisted.

"Who knows? Perhaps one day."

"Will we win again?"

"We won today. We will think about tomorrow when it comes."

And so she smiled, a warpath smile. She was hard. His women would not fail him.

"If we fight again," he told them, "we will be stronger. Rainbow and Five Wounds have returned from the buffalo grounds with their warriors. They will be here soon. Looking Glass and his people are coming."

"After he turned his back on us?" asked Strikes Standing, a woman of simple and steadfast loyalties.

"I have heard, grandmother, that the soldiers went to his village at Clear Creek. They drove Looking Glass and his people before them and tried to fire the tipis, which were wet and would not burn. Now Looking Glass will need us, as we need him."

"Then we will win, if we fight again?" asked Singing Beads.

"I say so."

"Will we go home then?"

"One day," he said. They all wanted to live something that could now only be sung. He had lied in his heart too long. He had to go outside and be alone. Strikes Standing, who knew him behind his words, followed.

"I will prepare the travois," she said.

"Yes. Be ready, grandmother. We will travel soon."

Then he walked past the fires where the braves danced, their painted faces made blood-red by the leaping flames. With eyes closed and pipe belching acrid smoke, Toohoolhoolzote sat, cross-legged, among them, imagining the Dream paradise to come.

Joseph went to the battleground. The dead were no longer leather dolls seen through a brass tube, but disfigured, swollen of face, without dignity. There was nothing good about death, and something lacking in the man who took life. In all his days he had killed no man, never brought the tomahawk down into the beating flesh, or loosed the man-killing arrow or bullet.

On his fingers Joseph totaled up the white casualties. Thirty-four dead, including Lieutenant Thaller. "I knew him alive," thought Joseph. "I wonder if he had a wife like Singing Beads; and children." He told the braves who searched the field for weapons flung away not to scalp or mutilate the dead. His own warriors he trusted completely, but not those who listened to Toohoolhoolzote.

Truly it was a great victory, and not one Indian life had been lost. It would live in memory and song. And yet he had heard tales from Indians who had been east and seen the great civil war between the white men. There the dead had lain in fly-buzzing heaps, too many to count or bury, battle after battle. White man's war was a game the Nez Percé had never played. The white man had more pieces to crowd upon the board. He could make up the rules as he went along, calling up men from Fort Walla Walla by steamer, calling them by the singing wire from south and west. The first play had been made and the Indians had won, but they might all die in the end with their hands stuffed with such victories.

Even now One-Armed Howard was planning, while the Indians celebrated as if the millennium had come. No sentinals were out. No watch was being kept. It would be all right, perhaps, for one night, but he must think. If he could take all the blame, he would accept it and hang. But Ollokot said it was too late. "Your back and mine are too broad to turn." Ollokot spoke truly. They were from the same branch, and they knew one another. Another choice was war. That had to be the wrong way, but he had already failed to prevent it when he had the chance. Then, was flight into the hills, away from the Wallawa, the only recourse? He could not reach out for one of these alternatives, saying with sureness, "This is good. This is what must be done," any more than he could return to his lodge and tell Singing Beads his decision, for in her eyes the rainbow, not the storm cloud, arched over him.

V
The Clearwater

Joseph sent scouts out at first light. They examined every trail, but Howard's army was nowhere in sight. Looking Glass and a few of his people were reported, however, and they arrived when the sun stood high overhead. They were unusually quiet, and many of them appeared to be stunned. The braves, announcing what they intended to do to their enemy, sounded more as if they spoke from duty than from conviction. All of them smelled of the smoke of their ravaged camp. At the head of the column, the old warrior led them with a shambling, bear-like gait. The white men had stolen his horse. He looked tired, ready for indefinite hibernation. But on seeing Joseph, he pulled his muscles together and stood erect.

"Looking Glass has come," he announced. "He will not leave again so long as he is alive."

"That is good, grandfather. We will need you."

Before nightfall, a dozen well-armed braves arrived from the buffalo ground. Rainbow and Five Wounds, boon companions on the hunt and in war, led them. Rainbow's face seemed chipped from flint and his eyes were shrewd, the smoldering eyes of a lynx. His every movement showed the agility of a body kept fit for a purpose, and that purpose was killing: buffalo, in time of peace; men, in time of war. Five Wounds was of the same cast, and upon his body his battling history was deeply chiseled. Yet, in spite of the ugliness of his scars, he had a certain determined dignity and a grace of carriage.

Joseph did not love these three, but he was glad of them now. When they met in council that night, along with Toohoolhoolzote and White Bird, it was still Joseph, backed by Ollokot, who spoke the final word. The enemy had been sighted. There was no great concentration of long knives, but troops were assembling, licking their wounds. All agreed that it was not wise to linger at White Bird Canyon. White Bird himself spoke out for the Old Lady's land, Canada. None had been there. His talk made it sound far away and very final. Backed up by Five Wounds and Rainbow, Joseph urged that they move out with stealth by night. They would withdraw into rough forest country with far-flung scouts and await General Howard's next move.

The Nez Percé set out under gusty showers which paused, renewed as downpours, and settled finally into a monotonous torrent of icy sprinkles. They went hunched to protect themselves, heads bent, arms crooked about muskets. When they finally camped, the rain fell with a soothing murmur on the tipis. The next day the icy rain still fell. The trail picked by Joseph led northwest toward the more westward curving bank of the Salmon River. He did not intend to cross but to move south from there into familiar territory, hoping to outlast the troops in the endless canyons of his Wallowa valley.

This time Joseph did not have the final word. White Bird and Looking Glass opposed him, and they were senior chiefs—White Bird because a crossing of the Salmon meant a step toward Canada; and Looking Glass because he hoped to find more of his people still camped upon the Clearwater. Scouts went out for news of Howard and learned that he was in the field with nearly three hundred fighting men, including the survivors of the White Bird fight. Two Gatling guns were with them, and a mountain howitzer, which the Indians feared. This news turned the council against Joseph's plan. They wanted the turbulent Salmon between themselves and the pursuers. With the rain still drenching down, they crossed it, losing several pack horses but no human lives. Days later, as they moved out toward the expanses of the Camas Prairies, they learned from returning scouts that Howard had arrived at the Salmon and built rafts to carry his men's supplies across, but the guide ropes had broken on the first attempt and Howard had given up. He'd turned back and was headed toward the White Bird, crossing many tortuous miles to the southeast.

Before women and children were committed to the wide-open crossing of the Camas Prairie, large scouting parties went out. A band led by Rainbow and Five Wounds intercepted ten troopers under Second Lieutenant Rains of Whipple's command near Craig's Mountain. In a thicket of willows and small pines at the foot of that mountain, the Indians waited for the clattering troopers. It was more like a firing squad than a fight. A few seconds of shooting and it was over, the troopers all dead, the Indians without a scratch.

Though the time seemed auspicious, they lingered another day, until July 5 by white man's reckoning, before crossing the Camas Prairie. At dawn they broke away from Piswah Illppilp Pap, the Place of Red Rock. The braves drove the stock ahead of them.

Midway, they encountered sixteen Mount Idaho volunteers led by D. B. Randall. These men were armed with Winchester and Henry repeating rifles, and Joseph guided the families and the stock away toward Rocky Canyon while Ollokot and the other war chiefs formed a half-mile line of mounted warriors as a screen. Into this screen Randall charged. The Indians opened to let him pass through, then closed. Randall's horse fell and he shouted out: "Boys, don't run! Let's fight em!" So, from a meager elevation, they fought on foot.

The Indians wished only to pass. They fired from a distance and the volunteers, called later in the press the "Brave Seventeen," fired back. Randall and another volunteer died. Two Indians were hit. One, Wounded Mouth, was carried to Joseph with a bullet in his chest. Joseph placed him on a travois padded with deerskins, but it did no good. Wounded Mouth died that night, the first Indian fatality in the Nez Percé war.

Once the stock and the Nez Percé families were safely past the embattled volunteers, the braves disengaged as more volunteers arrived with a Gatling gun. Fearing that this meant Howard was in close pursuit, Joseph allowed no respite throughout the afternoon. That night they arrived, exhausted, near the banks of the Clearwater. This was Looking Glass's home, and members of his scattered tribe came out to meet the refugees. Dried venison and serviceberries were doled out to those in need, and Joseph cut ridgepoles for the tipi skins. When Singing Beads began to prepare the meal, he took her by the arms and nodded to Strikes Standing.

"You'll need your strength for the baby and yourself," he told her. She insisted she was strong as a horse, two horses. "I'm glad," he replied. "I want you strong as three horses. Now sit. Take care of your baby. Tomorrow we will be on the trail."

But the next day they did not move. Horse racing took place. Parties went out hunting. Sentinels were posted, at Joseph's insistence, but it was not until evening, when mosquitoes hummed in golden clouds, that he could assemble the chiefs. Looking Glass was the last to appear.

As he arrived with his gliding, limping step, Joseph asked him, "Grandfather, what god protects you and your people?"

"I ask nothing from the gods," Looking Glass said.

Joseph was the first to address the gathering. His voice rose so slowly and carefully that some who did not know him thought him stupid. Once again he urged that a delegation be sent to Howard, in hopes of stopping the war. He offered to go alone if he had the backing of the others. But they were flushed with victory.

"Would you crawl like a tipi dog to the white man's

feet and lick his hand?" Looking Glass demanded. Throughout the lodge there was grunting accord. But Joseph continued and the chiefs listened, their faces stiff with silent opposition. He might have been talking to stones, and he knew it very well. Even Ollokot was against him.

"If you go, brother, the white chief will put you in jail."

"I would take that chance," Joseph replied.

"They would put you in a lodge with no windows and no smoke vent and there would be nothing to see and no way to get out."

It was Looking Glass who spoke for the others. His voice was deep and growling, full of thunder, as he began. "Joseph has told you his mind. Now hear mine. Joseph is a wise man, but his visions are not those of a warrior. In ways of war his tongue is not straight. Hear me, for I speak from many battles with the Shoshoni." In his pride, his face grew dark as jerked venison. A pulse pounded in his sweat-beaded brow. He spoke long, heroic thoughts. They worried Joseph, for he feared that even he would begin to follow that dangerous trail of words which lay end to end along the edge of a chasm. "We are men," Looking Glass told them. "We will not run away. This is our home. We will put our women and children safe away into the hills and then we will stand and fight. The right place to live is in the land of our fathers, and it is the right place to die."

"You are ready to die tomorrow?" Joseph asked him.

"Yes. Here. Tomorrow."

"But what if we die without accomplishing anything? You'll agree that would be stupid."

"It is better to die with a war whoop. It is better to die quickly from a bullet, than slowly from whiskey and disease." Looking Glass was raving now.

"Are you speaking for our wives and children, too?" asked Joseph.

Looking Glass rocked his head from side to side as though physically to wrestle free from Joseph's nets of logic. "We defeated One-Armed Howard before," he said. "We will defeat him again tomorrow. It will be the last battle."

"Yes. The last," said Joseph. "For the next will still be awaiting us. The white-eyes are many, like grains of sand in the river bed. They have guns and big-mouthed cannon to kill all the Nez Percé back to the ghosts of our grandfathers."

"Take care what you say, Joseph."

"Take care yourself, grandfather."

The chiefs were united behind Looking Glass. Toohoolhoolzote spoke wildly about the returning of the old ways. Indian gods would ride with them into battle and turn aside the bullets. They would sweep the white-eyes before them into the sea. White Bird spoke with less frenzy. His determination came from fear of hanging. If they would not flee north, then truly it was better to fight than to surrender meekly to the noose which would choke off a man's soul as well as his life. Though the others stood heavy and motionless, their fury was aroused. When it came time to vote, Joseph was alone against them all. Even Ollokot would not stand with him. He left the lodge so as not to declare himself, for his heart was with his brother but his blood was with the warriors.

That night the skies cleared and the stars looked down. Joseph walked late by the river, where the mists rose like phantoms. He thought of his father and the promises he had made. He thought of taking his family away from this madness and returning home. No one would notice one family of Indians traveling alone. But he could never leave his people—not one woman, not one child, so long as they remained alive.

Dawn began in the east like the blaze of a vast fire kindled beneath the edge of the earth. The day was hot and sunny from the start, and with the first dry warmth scouts began arriving. One-Armed Howard was near. He had with him men on foot and horse, soldiers, packers, volunteers. Adding them together in his mind, Joseph estimated the total at six hundred, three times the number of fighting braves in camp. Yet the village was at rest. Some were bathing in the river; others raced horses before the real heat began. Cooking fires rose from every tipi. When Joseph strode about urging them to be ready to leave, only his people listened. The people of White Bird, Toohoolhoolzote, and Looking Glass heard only their own chiefs, and for the most part were unaware of Howard's approach until a four-inch howitzer was rolled to the bluff above the camp. Out spat smoke and fire, announcing war and death to come. But it spoke too soon, before the troops were in position above the camp.

The Indian village lay in the narrow deep valley of the Clearwater, flanked on either side by steep pine-covered bluffs and opening at one end into a wider plateau. The howitzer was firing at long range down onto the camp before the troops had a chance to come up in force, let alone flank or surround the village. Toohoolhoolzote and his few warriors were the first into the fray, but they were quick enough to seize the lower bluffs and timber fringe above the river. Indians and soldiers alike, with no plan in mind, rushed to form a ragged crescent line pricked by the flash of musket fire. Mules brayed, the Indians whooped, the howitzer boomed too far away to contribute anything but noise. The soldiers dared not advance through open ground. The Indians dared not retreat, but dug in along the bluff. All day the sniping went on under a withering sun. The only immediate objective was a small water hole between the haphazard lines. The Nez Percé had the river at their backs and did not lack water, but the soldiers had only the tepid contents of their canteens. By afternoon, several soldiers had tried to reach the water hole. One crawled off wounded; two others died. It had not occurred to the troops until then that Indians might possess rifles with telescopic sights, let alone use them with such fatal accuracy.

Throughout the morning, Joseph organized the camp for flight if it became necessary. The other tribes were more inclined to listen to him now. Some loaded their travois. Many, trusting in their own chiefs, took no notice. By midday, nothing more could be done. Joseph returned to his tipi and saw that Strikes Standing and his own people had done what was necessary. He then proposed to find Ollokot at the battle line. "Nothing will happen to you," Singing Beads insisted.

"No. Nothing will happen to me today. I promise you that."

Death was an easy answer, but he could not afford such luxury while his people needed him. He had no difficulty finding Ollokot. He had dug in directly opposite their own part of the camp. There the air smelled of acrid cordite, of pulverized stone, and of death. Ollokot was lying flat against the bank when Joseph saw him first, and there was blood on the back of his neck. Joseph rushed to him with a cry of despair, thinking his brother had been killed, but Ollokot turned round at his approach with a burst of boyish laughter. His neck had been gnawed by horseflies.

"Their big-mouthed guns cannot reach us down here," he explained. "We can hardly find them with our rifles. It is a strange battle to go on so long." They talked little. These two could communicate like ants. They needed only to look at one another to know what was in the other's heart.

"Have many of ours been hit?" asked Joseph.

"No. A few, perhaps. It goes well. The white-eyes are thirsty."

"I will send food. If there are wounded, have them brought here." So that afternoon, with the help of a few of the older braves and Strikes Standing, Joseph carried up food and water to the warriors and took the wounded back. Between the river bank and the camp was open ground. There bullets hummed like spring bees. On Joseph's third trip, it was as though a branding iron suddenly touched his arm. He felt more surprise than hurt. A bullet had struck him, leaving a pink crevice in his arm. It filled with welling blood that ran down over his wrist. Death had touched him, but it was only a warning.

"I will bind it," said Strikes Standing.

"Not now, grandmother. Later."

"Hear me. You will grow faint." She took hold of his arm forcibly. He submitted as she bound the wound with trade cloth.

"Where would I be without you?" he said.

"Here, but dripping. There, that will do."

"Thank you, little mother."

"I am no one's mother," she reproached him. "I do what I can."

"You do more than I ask. You are the ridgepole that holds up my lodge. Believe that. Now go and be safe. I will come."

But she stayed with him, and together they went back and forth with the wounded. At first Joseph felt a stiffness in his legs. He had to make them move, chiding himself: "This old squaw has more courage in her big toe than you have in your belly." He was not a brave man in the sense that he lost all awareness of self in battle, but he managed to command his body. He moved back and forth through the bullets, not dragging the wounded, but carrying them gently so as not to aggravate their pain.

So it went throughout the dusty, stifling afternoon. No ground had changed hands when the sun finally set. Red and winking fires, friendly and hostile, glowed in the darkness, and nothing spoke of war except a soldier caught between the lines at the water hole with a bullet in his stomach. At regular intervals he screamed loudly and without shame, until it was dark enough for his comrades to carry him away.

Under the cliffs, the braves had scooped out a shelter where the chiefs could powwow during the fight. They met there at night, and Joseph spoke of withdrawing secretly before the fighting went from good to bad. He might have persuaded them, for all were weary from the long fight, had not a treaty Nez Percé, known among the whites as Joe Albert, deserted from Howard's force. He had been scouting for many days and now he had endured enough. The soldiers were discouraged, he reported. Another day and they would be finished.

This was all Looking Glass needed. He lifted his great head. In the manner of one who defies the hereafter, he threw up a square right hand, all puffed and muscled on the palm. He struck the fist down against his chest. "It is better to attack than retreat! Something has died in a warrior when he retreats. Tomorrow we will finish Howard. We will kill him and his long knives. We will cut them to bits!"

"You hate too much," Joseph told him.

The old warrior stared at him. The poison of rattlesnakes gleamed in his eyes. "And you hate too little, Joseph." The force of these words remained visible in the jut of his broad chin. It was no good arguing with such a one. Looking Glass listened to no one, and in the deadlock between them Joseph had no chance. The blood of the fighters was up, and they followed Looking Glass. Though outnumbered five to one and low on ammunition, they elected to fight again the next day until Howard was beaten forever.

For Joseph, it was a day and a night and a day that were all of one piece. He did not sleep, though his head felt big and hollow. Between his eyes, the bone and flesh seemed to be growing into one chunk of stone. Perhaps he had been wrong to try to take the safe way. Perhaps it was the coward's path. For Indians to hold their ground was an unheard-of thing. It must have sown doubt in the hearts of even the veterans among the whiteeyes. And as long as they fought, their women and children would know that all was well. No great misfortune could happen as long as their men were whole.

That second day of the Battle of the Clearwater started well enough. It was hot again. The soldiers hesitated to attack. Ollokot led one charge that nearly captured the big-mouthed gun, but during the night the soldiers had piled up rocks for shelter and the Indians were beaten back. By midday the sun scorched down, and still they fought for freedom, because without freedom their bodies might live for a time but their souls would die. "Howard will do well to fear them as long as they are above ground," Joseph thought with reluctant pride. But even as his hopes rose, he sensed a change, as imperceptible at first as a shift in atmospheric pressure. The river valley was a hearth over which the heat shuddered all day. The soldiers would have to take the water hole or die. Using the howitzer, they took it. That was no great affair and it cost them dear. Neither the loss of the water hole nor the shortage of ammunition worried Joseph. They never had enough bullets. It was the way the braves had begun drifting back to camp, for a drink, for food, not tearful or defeated, but simply weary of war. It did no good for Toohoolhoolzote to rage at them of the old days returning, or for Looking Glass to shame them with the name "Coward." They had been brave men fighting fearful odds for a day and a half and now they were tired.

In mid-afternoon the First Cavalry, commanded by Captain James Jackson, attacked the right flank of the Nez Percé line. There Wahlitits and Five Wounds rallied their warriors. Then the soldiers attacked all up and down the line, and the howitzer was rolled into a new position. Its first shell, exploding among the tipis, was the signal for disaster. The rout was complete. Squaws and old men bolted into the river. Those who had not heeded Joseph's warning left everything . . . clothes, tipis, bubbling stew pots. While Joseph herded the pack animals together, saving what he could, the other chiefs tried to rally the warriors in front of the dismantled village, but the explosion of shells, the shrieking of women and children and horses, unmanned them entirely. They plunged into the river, and helplessly the war chiefs followed.

By the time the troops stumbled down from the bluffs, the Indians were in full flight, strung out in a fast-moving column of warriors, squaws, ponies, pack horses loaded with goods and clinging children, dogs running alongside, mixed in with old men and boys. Warriors brought up the rear. Joseph ranged round the column, keeping it together, seeing that no one fell behind.

With two days of grinding battle behind them and a river between them and the fleeing enemy, the soldiers did not follow. They had wounded to care for and the dead to bury. First the white corpses, then the red, went into the ground—about thirty in all; no one was ever quite sure. The wounded were taken back to hospital.

The Indian wounded were tied to jouncing travois to survive their pain without medication, or to take the easier way and die. Most of these were in Joseph's care. He took them water and what food he could find, and he dressed their wounds with herbs as Strikes Standing advised.

"Father, father," one of the wounded called to him, "what kind of white man's hell is this?"

"You will be all right. We are looking after you," he replied. What else could he say to one twice his age who called him Father? Yet some would die, for death in the end is father to all men.

The Nez Percé trekked most of the night, stopping toward morning but without setting up tipis or cooking food. The following day, heading northeast with cavalry scouts behind them, they crossed Lolo Creek at noon and by dusk had climbed the steep bluffs of Weippe Prairie, a favorite summer rendezvous among the Nez Percé in times of peace. Here the wild camas lilies grew. The entire prairie was carpeted a bluish sheen with these delicate flowers, and their bulbs were like raw onions. Cooked as the Indians liked them, they were sweet. Joseph remembered happy times in the past when the women and girls had dug up the bulbs with curved sticks while the men and boys hunted and gambled away the days. White traders had come to sell liquor. They'd had good times. But there were no whites there now, and no time for dancing. There was very little time even to dig bulbs, though all were hungry.

The Army was on their trail and few of the warriors believed they could defeat them now. Toohoolhoolzote was silent and brooding. In council they would have to decide what to do: stand and fight and probably die, or run away. And if they ran, where would they go? The chiefs met around a blazing fire which turned their faces into grim red masks.

White Bird spoke first. His hands rose and fell in limp gestures of uncertainty. He was troubled and sad. He had seen Modocs hanged when he was a young warrior, hanged by the white men for doing less than the Nez Percé had already done. If they gave themselves up to the white men now, the chiefs would surely hang, and their people would go in chains to Indian territory in the south, there to wither and die and trouble the white men no longer. But if they stayed in their homelands, sooner or later they would have to fight again. He wanted them to flee beyond the mountains, beyond the deserts of the horned toad and the lizard, to go as far away from their homeland as the eagle flies. They could go toward the lands of ice and snow, through the country of the friendly Flatheads. That was the quickest way into the Land of the Old Lady, where Sitting Bull had found a refuge. This was the way White Bird would go, and there were those who stood with him.

Then Joseph once again offered to parley alone with the whites. "What do we fight for, if not for our homeland?" he asked. But few listened.

Looking Glass stood up. His face was the hue of distant mountains, and he gave Joseph a derisive look. "May the Great Spirit help you," he said. "Your tongue is the strongest part of you." Then he described the buffalo country in Montana. He said the Crow Indians were friendly and would hunt with them. They would eat meat every day. Their ponies would grow fat. Even the whites were friendly there. A doctor in Missoula had treated his eyes. No soldiers would follow them, for the Lolo Trail through the Bitterroots was hard. After much confident talk, he proposed they all go that way. If trouble developed, they could turn north as White Bird suggested and join Sitting Bull in Canada.

Looking Glass had spoken. He folded his arms, and with a crushing glance he dared a long pause. He won through it in silence. All tongues were bound except Joseph's, who spoke because things had to be said even if they were not heard.

"Do you think, grandfather," he began, "that the white men are from different tribes as we are? They are one tribe. On this side of the Bitterroots and on the other, they are the same people with the same chief. That is their strength and weakness. Their doctors may put magic drops in our eyes, but they will not welcome us beyond the mountains even if we smile and bring them beaver skins." Looking Glass stared at him, as did all the other chiefs. In their bright feathers, they were a flock of furious, fighting birds. Still, things had to be said. "Grandfather, every blade of grass has its place, and there it draws its strength. Just so, everyone is rooted in the earth. Uproot him, and that man will die. Uproot a tribe, and that tribe will wither and vanish. Just so, we must stay. In the end we will regret leaving. We will never come home." He could not sway Looking Glass. It was like arguing with a tree. Looking Glass did not even bother to argue back. He simply listened and then talked again in a cold tone as if Joseph had never spoken.

Joseph knew that to press his desire for a powwow with One-Armed Howard might lead to tribal war. This was too great a risk. Nor would he think of weakening the whole by separating his people from the rest. Like black ants struggling through the dust with eggs bigger than themselves, they would go, all together, through the mountains. Let it be. He would say no more. When it came time to elect a war chief over all the Nez Percé, only Looking Glass was mentioned, and to this Joseph gave assent. Their one hope was in unity.

His last gesture toward peace before starting the long trek north was to send out Kulkulsuitim as a messenger to Howard. Perhaps if the General sent back assurances, there might yet be a meeting. But hostile Indian scouts employed by the Army fired on the messenger from a distance and drove him away. From that moment on, the point of turning back had passed. Home, the Wallowa he loved, lay west and south, but Joseph turned from it now with the others. He could not desert them. When the fighting was done, they would need him, so he went to his tipi and gathered his family about him. There was a long and difficult trail ahead, he told them, but at the end, somewhere at the end, they would find peace and a home.

On the morning of July 16, high summer, the Nez Percé were as ready as they would ever be for the long flight. They still had two thousand horses and pack animals, more than ample for their braves and for those possessions not left behind at the Clearwater. Travois had been cut for the wounded. Joseph sat his appaloosa at the head of the expectant column. Spring Song was beside him. She squeezed his hand. "The warriors have elected Looking Glass," she said. "But the people still call you Father." Knowing this to be so, Joseph began to sing the old chant, a song of home. Other voices joined him as he ranged along the straggle of two hundred warriors and five hundred and fifty old men, women, and children. These were all the Nez Percé who still lived in freedom, and the singing lifted them from terrible darkness. Then Joseph raised his arm, for in peace he remained their leader. There would be many times in the future when he would recall this moment of commitment and ponder on it.

They began to move slowly across the Weippe Prairie, where, seventy-two years before, his grandfathers had welcomed the first white men, Lewis and Clark. What had the years done to them? No matter; their bones were rolled and could not be picked up again.

Ollokot rode up beside him, his pony stepping sideways, wanting to gallop. "Brother, it will be a bad day," he said. They looked at the thunderclouds building up over the Bitterroot Mountains.

"A very bad day," replied Joseph. "I feel in my heart we will never come this way again." It was hard to imagine his beloved Wallowa cut off from him forever as surely as the legendary days of Coyote.

"I say we will return," Ollokot assured him. "Grandfather, we will die on the land that gave us birth. I feel it."

The long column wound down from the Weippe Prairie in silence. The wounded lay tight-lipped on their jogging travois. It was a deadly trail for them. The women went with heads bowed, heavily laden, their children and dogs padding beside them. The mounted warriors flanked their people. Their brows were set and they looked fiercely about. A tradition was being shattered, and it could not be lightly done.

No one looked back. Ahead, the Bitterroots built up, a vast and forested wilderness. Storm clouds towered above them. A prolonged peal of thunder rolled down from the mountains like the rumble of a runaway wagon on a stony road. It was a summons to Joseph. Yet always in his heart he yearned for home—the Wallowa, beautiful valley of the wind.

VI
The Bitterroots

The mountain cold and rain came down to meet them. The trail turned to mud under their feet. The going was slow, and, to make matters worse, Howard's Indian scouts, wearing the blue sash of stripes and stars, were close behind them. Wahlitits and Rainbow, with sixteen warriors, turned back to set an ambush. They slowed the pursuit, but they were too angry at these Christian Nez Percé who hunted their own people, and they fired upon them before they were well in range. Only a Kamiah Indian, John Levi, was killed, and the cavalry was warned.

By late afternoon the path had begun to climb. The slope steepened and the pine forests closed about them. Joseph's spirits rose as he feasted his eyes upon the richness of the unaxed forest. Mile upon mile was untouched as the Great Spirit had conceived it—older, vaster than the memory of tribes, older than the buffalo and the white man. Here were no rutted wagon roads, no fences, no cabins; only the countless trees. They were as mothers to the tribe. They meant freedom still.

Here dwelt the elk and the moose and the mountain cougar, the deer already turned red with summer. Here fell the fast clear streams. Higher up dwelt the mountain goats where the trees broke down and the views went on forever. Up toward these high places the Nez Percé made their way, Joseph driving them. They pressed through log-strewn tunnels of green, over the needle-hushed carpet of the forest floor. Though the great tree butts were dark with the rain which still fell in a monotonous torrent, there was no mud. The path remained clean and springy from the long-decayed logs and the pine needles which lay there, years deep.

For the next three days they walked and rode steadily and swiftly. Each day took on a tortuous repetition: a baby crying to begin with, some talk, some song, then the muffled beat of hoofs. Toward dusk, more children would be crying and there would be questions about a campsite and where to find water and game. The water came incessantly from the sky. They rode and walked in it by day and slept in it at night, so they need only suck at their blankets or buckskin shirts to still their thirst. But game was nowhere to be seen. There was nothing ahead or behind but the sea of pines until the far blue peaks marked the buffalo plains beyond seeing.

By the fifth day, their pride was gone. This had never been a hunting party stripped for fast travel, and now it was a weary rabble clawing its way through wilderness and leaving a trail of debris and dead horses. No fires would burn, but they began butchering ponies as soon as they went lame. The flesh was eaten raw. All the time, the pace grew slower because of the stragglers, and the wounded lashed to jolting, mud-caked travois. Disgusted, Looking Glass rode ahead with his war party, looking for Assiniboines who might attack them. Joseph was left to manage the people and the pack animals. Often the trees grew so thick that the travois and the packs jammed between trunks. At best, they clattered over fallen limbs. The earth had become a boneyard of trees, unburied skeletons over which the horses could or would not jump. If the trees could, Joseph wondered, would they bury their dead?

More horses fell, their legs or spirits broken. Those that pressed on were bruised and skinned by the rough trunks and the rawhide switches of the Indians who forced them forward. Higher up, where the trees thinned, the ground was covered with great stones which suggested the ruins of a lost city cast down from the skies. Still, they pressed forward, along the rims of deep precipices, over steep ridges, while the rain poured incessantly. No choice remained; it was press forward or die.

Joseph, with Strikes Standing, Ollokot, and the braves who stayed loyal to him, labored almost without sleep to find and clear a path. He worked with muscles which had been weary so long they had stopped feeling pain. "This is the way it is with the hunted stag," he thought, escaped for the moment into some covert, breathing hard, wanting to lie down, but knowing that the pursuit was close behind.

"Is your horse lame?" Ollokot asked him. It was now the sixth day in the Bitterroots.

"It is only a stiffness, I think. I'll lead him. He may warm up with the sun." Throughout the morning the horse followed him, still limping, his head now and then knocking softly against Joseph's back at a faltering step. Not until night did Joseph discover the reason: a long green thorn like a splinter of jade. "You are a brave and patient friend," he said, drawing the thorn. "And you, too," he said to the old dog, who limped from age alone. "I would let you ride if there was a place. We all can't ride. Even Singing Beads carries her baby now." His wife never complained, never fell behind, but she was breathing hard. He knew she was tired—tired and torn inside in a way no man could really understand.

On the seventh day, as they were nearing the land of the buffalo, the pace eased. Their scouts had learned earlier that a young Bannock warrior named Buffalo Horn, who hated all Nez Percé, had joined Howard and, with a Major Mason, led the Army's advance party. At the Bent Horn turn in the trail, Ollokot had lain in wait with his braves where the timber was thick. There had been a fierce fight, and now the returning scouts said the pursuit had fallen far behind.

One of the wounded braves and an old woman had died. That night Joseph took time to bury them secretly beneath scattered pine needles so that the Bannocks would not unearth them for trinkets or to violate the warrior's body so that it might wander blind and impotent in the spirit world to come. Joseph ordered the braves out to cut ridgepole pines, and for the first time on the Bitterroot trail they crept into tipis. For the first time Joseph really slept, with the rain sweeping on the buffalo skins and the big drops hissing into the banked fire.

Next morning they pulled down the skins, leaving the tipi poles standing. During the night the skies had cleared, and from their camp they could see mountains all about like a green sea, turbulent but frozen. Above them the sky was blazing blue. Once he had dreamed of walking on such mountain peaks, but no more. He would be content with the open plains, the warm canyon bottoms.

From this point on, the trail led down, widening all the way. Looking Glass rode back along the column, telling the people that by nightfall they would be in open country full of game and white men. In Montana he was a friend of the whites. They must harm no white man there and they must leave the cattle alone. The war was to be left behind in Idaho. A new life was beginning.

So they followed Lolo Creek through opening valleys. Here deer grazed and the pine forests were broken by meadows, deep green in midsummer. It was not home, but it would do. It would do for a while, and as they settled down beside the Lolo hot springs that night, Joseph felt hope return for the first time. The magic waters entered him and gave him peace.

Next morning they moved on with braves riding the flanks, hunters now rather than scouts, and it was with complete surprise that they arrived at Fort Fizzle. It wasn't called by any name at that time, for it was only a corral of rough-cut timber two feet high, around which both whites and Indians were swarming.

The Nez Percé column pulled up short, the chiefs riding ahead. They were puzzled at first. Only when the men in the fort began crouching down behind the low wall, their rifle barrels glinting over the top rail, was their purpose clear.

"They mean to stop us," exclaimed Looking Glass, full of outrage and affront.

With his long glasses, Joseph identified Whitebilly Silver Thorn among the defenders. A half-breed and a thief, they'd met him far back on the Lolo Trail. He must have brought the news of the Nez Percé outbreak.

"Let us ride over them," suggested Toohoolhoolzote, and some of the war chiefs grunted agreement. But Looking Glass had been declared leader over all, and he still thought of this land as friendly. He would parley.

It was not that easy. The garrison of Fort Fizzle was commanded by Captain Charles Rawn, "I" company, Seventh Infantry. He had under his command twenty-five regulars and twice that many civilian volunteers, and he would not believe the Nez Percé came in peace to Montana. He stalled for time, and under the white flag nothing was decided that first day. Two hostile camps winked at one another through the night of July 25 in Lolo Canyon. The next day Captain Rawn offered to let the tribes pass if they surrendered their arms. Looking Glass, remembering the Columbia River war, where the whites had promised the same, only to hang the unarmed braves, would not have it. Another day passed and another conference was held. This time Joseph spoke for the Indians. "Joseph holds up his hand to the sun, and offers his other hand to his white brothers in the Salish land. May the Great Spirit wither within him when he breaks his word—Joseph, who has never broken his word." Still Captain Rawn held out. He wanted someone higher up to give him orders, but there was no one higher up. Many of the volunteers relied on Joseph's pledge, or, out of fear, told themselves they did and began to disappear.

That night the Nez Percé chiefs conferred among themselves. They were getting nowhere with this Rawn. The sight of the Bitterroot Indians darting and dancing in the firelight of the white camp, their shoulders shining, infuriated them. What cowards to dance their war dance behind white men's guns! To make matters worse, Whitebilly Silver Thorn came out to warn the Nez Percé not to harm the white men in Montana. White Bird, looking trail-weary and old, had begun to remind Joseph of his own father in that chief's last years. It was he who rebuked Silver Thorn. "Harken. You may tell the Salish braves that White Bird has heard the words of Whitebilly Silver Thorn and knows his evil heart and crooked tongue. The day will come soon when your Salish chiefs will leave their land as we have left ours, with tears in their eyes."

That was well and wisely said. Joseph added nothing to it. "Why do we Indians always divide against one another," he wondered. "Why are these Salish Indians, who need us as we need them, against us now? It must be the cleverness of the whites, who do not have to kill their enemies but get them to kill each other." He would not let it go that far, not this time. In the last council that followed, he urged that they pass round the camp. There were paths to the bluffs above. No blood need be shed, white or Indian. Looking Glass, still feeling that he had friends in Montana, agreed that this was truly spoken.

Others disagreed, particularly the younger warriors, led by Wahlitits, who had begun the trouble. "No fighting," Looking Glass told him, and when Wahlitits would not speak, Looking Glass's whip cut him. Red Moccasin Tops came at him with a drawn knife, but the old chief was quicker than he looked, and spun round with cocked carbine. He would have killed the young brave if Joseph had not intervened. "Enough of this! We have enough bloodshed without killing each other."

Before dawn, the camp was in motion. They took to the ridge above the trail and, with the braves riding as a screen, passed Fort Fizzle by. A few of the soldiers jumped over the low wall as though to charge. Looking Glass waved his hat at them. "Don't shoot. Let the white man shoot first. Any Indian who fires first is a dead man."

There was not a gun discharged that morning. The Nez Percé had an easy victory. Most of them took it as a mistake, or at most a joke, for only Joseph saw the handwriting on the wall. The newspapers all over Montana and the East commented with amused disgust, and the legend of "Fort Fizzle" was born.

After Fort Fizzle, no one stood in their way, and the Nez Percé proceeded slowly down the river valley. During the day they hunted for deer. It took more time than in mating season, when a doe could be attracted by striking antlers together in imitation of fighting buck, but game was plentiful. Dusk began early on this side of the Bitterroots. They traveled in shadow while the sky still blazed with light, and camp was made long before the night.

Joseph feared that Howard would overtake them or, by sending messages over the click-clack and the singing wires, have them intercepted. But Looking Glass would not move any faster. They had no enemies here, he insisted. When they passed Fort Owen, crowded with settlers, he and his braves rode up jauntily to the walls and reassured the families crouching inside that no person, no property, in Montana would be touched so long as the Nez Percé were left in peace. They were further delayed by the arrival of a war-bonneted delegation from the Flathead chief, Eagle in the Light. Their spokesman was Horn-Hide Dresser, a gaunt and gloomy old medicine man with a hawk nose as brown and thin as a bone turned up in damp soil. Scalped long ago, he wore in place of hair a rag of beaver pelt over the scar. In garbled words and hand signs, he told of the Flathead troubles with the whites. "If Joseph will come with his people, two hundred warriors await only the wave of his hand to spring up like the buffalo wolf and tear apart the soldiers and drive them from the land."

"We are not looking for war. We must find a home," Joseph told him.

"Then come. We are friends who will lead you through our land to the Land of the Old Queen. Perhaps we will go with you, for the white man says to us, 'This land is mine. The trees are mine. The mountains, prairies, streams are mine. The deer, the fish, the buffalo; even the grass is mine from where the sun rises in the morning to where it goes down in the night.' The black robes say, 'Give us land so we can put up big tipis to the white man's God. Then he will come and smile on your people.'"

Again, in council, White Bird favored accepting the invitation. West of Flathead Lake lay the shortest route to Canada. "We have tramped enough toward the sun's rising," he said. "Let us join Sitting Bull and Eagle in the Light while time remains."

Looking Glass listened silently; he sat in council like a boulder. "White Bird," he said finally, "you sit on my leg."

"Some would say your leg kicks," replied the chief.

This time the council was divided. Toohoolhoolzote, perhaps because Horn-Hide Dresser was, like himself, an exhorter and medicine man, perhaps because of visions he said he had seen, stood with White Bird. Most of the young braves backed Looking Glass in his desire to head for the Big Hole and the Yellowstone. There the Crows would befriend them, he said. He did not trust these Bitterroot Indians, since he had seen them with the whites at Fort Fizzle.

In the end, Joseph was called upon to break the deadlock. For some time he stood lost in deep thought. His lips moved as if spelling something out in his mind. On the one hand, there was safety in Canada, strength in having Indian allies—and yet, it was far beyond hope of returning. "I am tired," he began. "I am tired of shedding white man's blood, for though his blood runs downhill in rivers and he falls like grass in a storm of wind and hail, I see ten white men rise in the place of every one who dies. It would do no good to carry our war to your people. Go back to them and tell the warriors the words of their friend, Thunder Traveling to Loftier Mountaintops. Tell them not to heed the voices of danger that tell them to go to war with the white men, for they are wrong. The white man is mighty, and he has a savage God. Together they are strong. No matter whether they are wrong or right, it is for the Indian his death song. In the end it will be better for them to accept the white man's wrongs. Then they will not be like Joseph and his people, hunted like wolves, without a home. We will go to the Big Hole as Looking Glass wishes."

"Evil is this day and place for White Bird and his people," said that chief, "when he knows that he is doing wrong to them. But so that others cannot call him or his warriors cowards, White Bird goes."

So it was decided. The Flatheads withdrew, surprised and disappointed. It remained only for Joseph to urge haste. "We have beaten back the white man each time, but we are fugitives and they are locusts. They grow while we decrease. They have their click-clacks to talk to one another at great distance, and their paper for leaving word behind them. We will follow Looking Glass, but quickly. Hear me, Looking Glass. We must go with wings."

Surprised by this unexpected support, Looking Glass agreed without hesitation. They would head directly for the Big Hole, follow the Big Hole River down to the

Jefferson Fork of the Missouri, and move into the wild Yellowstone country. There on the edge of the buffalo plains, far from the fenced farms of the white man, they could settle and be forgotten. It was easier than going all the way to Canada.

The plan sounded all right around the council fire. Looking Glass spoke without fear. Joseph went to his lodge and slept soundly. But in the morning he was full of doubt. It was a night plan. Now that he had slept, he could see more clearly, and he observed uneasily the leisure with which the camp broke up for the trail. They moved slowly through short-grass country. A featureless expanse rose toward fanged mountains. They saw their first prairie wolves and the owls that burrowed into the ground. There, too, were the distant cabins of the white men and the wooden barriers set up to keep their cattle from running free.

The pace infuriated Joseph. What was Looking Glass up to? What new maggot had hatched in his brain? Joseph rode up to him. Looking Glass heard him out with the maddening invulnerability of the ignorant.

"Joseph," he said, "you talk like the crow. Peck, peck, peck. Always uneasy, always pecking. I tell you there is no need to hurry. The rear guard came to me at dawn. One-Armed Howard is not pursuing us. And remember, I have friends here." When reminded of the telegraph, he said, "Then we will cut the singing wires. We need not fear One-Armed Howard. Let him fear us, Joseph."

"You have the courage of a blind man, Looking Glass. Take care, or you will destroy us all with blind courage," Joseph admonished him. But all they saw and heard that day and the next supported Looking Glass. Few whites were about, and those who were seemed undisturbed by the Nez Percé migration. Some were ready to trade for horses or buffalo robes.

When the Indians arrived near Stevensville, a regular stop on buffalo hunts, the braves rode into town behind Looking Glass. Most houses were closed and shuttered. Women and children huddled inside the small stockade, but shops were open, never to better business. Joseph took Spring Song and rode after the braves. Besides the Nez Percé already there, he saw more Flathead Indians than whites. They were armed and they gloomily patrolled the town. "Against us," thought Joseph. "It is as Looking Glass said; they are against us too."

With Spring Song, he entered the general store—a marvelous place. No Indian, not even a chief, could deny that. The ceiling was hung like a stalactited cavern with plows, chains, axes, harnesses, cheap shoes. The walls were lined with barrels, molasses, nails, brown sugar. A small sad clerk with tin cuff links and plastered hair seemed anxious to please even Indians so long as they were armed. He was sorry, he said, he couldn't take buffalo robes. Summer robes always seemed to be stolen, he explained, but he'd sell most anything for cash or horses. "White flour." He let a handful smoke through his fingers. "Blackstrap nigger-heel molasses, mighty tasty. Dollar a bottle." A couple of braves sat on the floor downing molasses by the quart and looking puzzled that it didn't hit home as whiskey did. Toohoolhoolzote was there. He'd filled his pipe bag with white man's weed, and his brown, red-veined face softened with the first long pulls at his pipe.

"Brown sugar for your squaw, Injun?" the clerk inquired of Joseph.

He hated "squaw" from a white man. He kept his mouth tight shut, but his eyes were shouting.

"Sorry, no whiskey today," said the clerk. "Sure you don't want brown sugar? Going fast."

"Bullets," Joseph told him.

"Mighty dear today. Dollar apiece."

Joseph placed a twenty-dollar gold piece on the counter.

Some other Indians settled for brown sugar. Five of them shared out a ten-pound bag of raw sugar and ate it on the spot while the clerk gave a hoarse, wheezing laugh that made his belly go up and down and his eyes fill with tears. "Jesus, sweet Jesus," he said, "how the money rolls in."

One merchant traded off whiskey for horses. There were tense moments between Nez Percé and Flatheads. Guns were pointed but not fired.

"You Flatheads are no longer our brothers," Toohoolhoolzote said. "Your dream of being friends with the white man will fade like the summer snow. Their faces and tongues are like a day in early spring. Sometimes the sun shines warm, but soon come gales of wind and ice. You Flathead warriors, you will soon know what we know about friendly white men."

Together with Joseph, Looking Glass patrolled the

streets. Drunks were bundled off to camp. Unruly ones Joseph admonished: "Shoot one farmer and you make twenty new enemies." He had to pull curious braves away from the glass windows of houses. "Windows are for looking out, not in," he told them.

Returning to camp, Joseph found that his tribe had been joined by a mixed bunch of Snake and Bannock warriors, off on a hunt and seeking companionship on the trail. "We're at war with the whites," he told them. They shrugged that off. Among them was a short, talkative brave, Lean Elk, more often called Poker Joe for his gambling with the whites. Poker Joe had humorous sardonic eyes that believed nothing and feared less. He had a way of leaning forward as he walked. He was a tracker, and after he'd injured himself in the Bitterroots, the whites there had accused him of having been wounded fighting against Howard. Very well, let it be. If the Nez Percé would have him, he would go along. He knew the country east of the Bitterroots. Joseph looked for a double motive in his face and found nothing beyond his words. "Good. We will smoke the pipe together," Joseph said. They would need Poker Joe in the days to come more than he could imagine.

During the next several days they proceeded at Looking Glass's leisurely pace, no more than twelve miles with each sun. Here and there they traded at stores. Once Toohoolhoolzote's braves rifled a deserted cabin owned by one Myron Lockwood. On hearing the news, Looking Glass made them take three of their own ponies, brand them with the Lockwood iron, and loose them in Lockwood's corral in appeasement. From then on, Toohoolhoolzote camped apart with his braves.

"You have made an enemy of that one," Joseph said.

"That Dreamer," replied Looking Glass with scorn. "Better that we stay friends with these white men . . . for now."

Joseph regarded the whites of Montana only as spies. Every man, every woman, every child, pale faces looking out of doorways, pale faces behind shutters, all were enemies, sending their whispers over the singing wire.

Those were daytime fears. At night, Joseph lodged with Ollokot. The two families became a small world, so happily complete there seemed no room for outside threat. It was good to have such a brother as Ollokot, faithful as his old dog, when faith was needed, yet with a good kind of pride which he carried always. It was good, too, to have such women as Strikes Standing and Singing Beads. Even a chief had no right to such fortune. Then there were his daughters and Ollokot's little boys. They'd discovered a cinnamon cub on the forest's fringe who was as curious about them as they were about his clownish rompings. "Ayee," Joseph called to get their attention. "Children, stay close. There are grandfather bears about. Spring Song, I have seen their marks." The grass not far from camp was slashed away where bears had dug for camas roots, and on the ridge pines were claw marks too high for a full-grown cinnamon. A grizzly had been marking his territory. "Stay close, children." He kept his carbine in his lap, wishing it were a big-bored buffalo gun. It took many shots with the carbine to stop a grizzly, and a grizzly in the open could move faster than a buffalo.

No bear came near while the light held. "I'm a worrier," Joseph said. "I make up worries." Then at dusk, when the two families were gathered in the firelight, the horses began to whinny and stamp. He wondered if scouts were out. Could it be that One-Arm had caught up with them? No, old One-Arm was too clever to panic horses, but perhaps there were older enemies—night hunters, slipping through shadows. Next the camp dogs took up the complaint, howling like the wolves they were in part. From the dark forest came roars and clashings, short bursts of fury.

"They play with the grandfather bear," said Ollokot.

"A game that may kill them," replied Joseph. He called his own dog, who was too old to win at such sport, and presently the dog came. His ears were flat against his skull and his bony tail was clamped low between his legs. Another dog loped by, ki-yipping from a wound that had laid bare his entire flank.

Joseph grabbed for his carbine, levering a cartridge into the chamber. As he did so, the grizzly reared high in the flickering shadows. He was hump-shouldered, red-eyed, yellow-fanged, and big as the killer god for which he was named, Simahichen. Joseph hustled the others behind him. Ollokot had a knife, but no gun. He stood at his brother's side for honor's sake, though he could do very little. The bear swayed slightly, forward and back, snapping the air with fury. The Indians were frozen with fear, and something intangible held the bear back as well.

Minutes passed. The fire, which had been crackling high, began to fall. There was no more wood. "O Simahichen," Joseph said, "if you do not leave us before it grows too dark to aim, I will have to shoot you. I have no wish to kill my forest brother. Leave us." The bear clawed the earth but did not approach. "Bear, if you stay, it is because you wish to die." Doubting that he had put a shell into the breech, Joseph drew down the Winchester's lever only a fraction of its arc. The shell was there. He clicked it back, and as though that metallic click had undone a great spring, the bear's bulk suddenly hurtled through the moon glow. Joseph fired once, twice, then fell as a claw razored through the buckskin of his shirt. He was somersaulted backwards. His gun was lost but he heard it exploding somewhere. Ollokot was firing point-blank, and the bear, wheezing and panting, gave a piteous moan of pain. It swayed helplessly with its hind legs spread sideways. Then it began to cry like a baby, and Ollokot approached it. He spoke harshly, "Now you are a coward, Simahichen. You only feign bravery. Had you defeated me, I would have died in silence like a warrior. You whimper like a child." But Joseph revered the bear and apologized for the rudeness of the killing. Retrieving the rifle, he took away the bear's suffering with a shot between the eyes. Slowly the bear collapsed forward, yielding up its life with a final wheeze as it landed flat. The legs jerked once, a last flicker of the nerves beneath the fur, and then it lived no more.

"May he speak well of us in the next world," said Joseph.

His family crowded round. This was a great thing, the killing of a grizzly. Singing Beads brought herbs for Joseph's arm, but he told her to save them, it was but a scratch. While Ollokot began skinning the dead bear, the whole tribe gathered round. They heaped up the fire. They danced. It was useless for Joseph to order them to sleep, to save their strength for the trail. Such moments were rare and had to be celebrated.

A few braves danced all night, and those that slept dreamed of bears and blood. On the trail next day there was great unrest, by no means eased by their arrival at the sacred medicine tree of the Salish and Sahaptin peoples. The stately yellow pine had stood alone for all of living memory with a huge mountain sheep's horn imbedded high in its trunk. Here was great medicine and here Looking Glass's exhorter, Culculhensah, donned his buffalo-head mask and bearskins to preach haste to all who would listen. Wahlitits rode his war pony around the uneasy circle, calling out that he had seen himself killed in a dream. "I will be killed!" he shouted. "I am ready to die. I do not care. I shall welcome death. We are all going to die!" Lone Bird told of dreams warning of disaster if they did not make haste. "Death stalks our trail," he shouted.

A look of doubt came into Looking Glass's face. He

glanced uneasily at the braves, then scoffed at their fears. "Where is this death? The sun is bright. The fields are green. I see no enemy, no One-Armed Howard. Who has seen this death?" Even as he spoke, Bannock braves were spotted watching them from afar.

"They are spies for One-Arm," exclaimed Lone Bird.

"Hunters, nothing more," replied Looking Glass.

"I have spoken with them," said Lone Bird. "They say they hunt, but they speak as white men. They say 'By Jesus' and 'God damn.' They are spies."

Looking Glass's face darkened and he looked ready to attack the young brave with his bare hands. "Grandfather," he said derisively, "you have not said anything, but already you have spoken too much. You know what I mean. If you enjoy what you are doing enough to fight about it, go on, speak. If not, be silent." He stared toward the sun's rising. His glance swept like the aiming of a rifle to the far horizon. "Tomorrow at the Big Hole we will rest. That is what I, Looking Glass, intend. I have spoken."

They traveled all afternoon to get there. The travois made of lodgepoles were lashed to the ponies. They moved slowly and left a clear trail. One-Arm has no need of scouts, thought Joseph. Anyone could follow such a trail, and there was no way to cover it over. He felt sure of disaster, but was not clear from which direction it would come, or when. He told himself, "I am not a coward, but I see things clearly. There are many riding beside me now who will never see another full moon."

He even had a horrid sense of those who would die. It was as though he could see it in their faces. He had seen it in Wahlitits, a clear and glowing aura; and there were others among those who could still laugh.

VII
The Big Hole

Looking Glass and his favorite braves rode ahead to pick a campsite. Toward evening on the seventh of August, Joseph brought the Nez Percé people down through brush, cottonwood, and dwarf ash to the old Salish campsite known as Ishkumzizlakik Pah, the Place of the Ground Squirrel. Here the buffalo trail and Ruby Creek joined. Here Nez Percé hunting parties were accustomed to join with Flatheads and Shoshonis in chasing the buffalo and fighting the Piegans and Bloods. This time they camped on the western edge of the flat prairie of the Big Hole. Joseph would have preferred a more open site, for there were dense concealing thickets of willow along the stream. To the northwest were pine-covered mountains breaking down into sagebrush near the camp where two large fir trees stood side by side like lonely sentinels above the valley floor. Upstream from the camp, timber thrust into the valley, and the slope was gentle compared to the mountains behind. There the Big Hole River had cut into the soil, forming a high bluff over its channel.

"This is a bad place," Joseph said to Ollokot after they had scanned all the cover near the camp. They were setting up ninety-four tipis in the shape of a flight of geese, Joseph's tribe at the head, White Bird's forming one wing, and Looking Glass's the other. But there were good reasons for pausing here, too—reasons that had to do with comfort rather than safety. All about were the young lodgepole pines, so necessary for erecting a decent lodge that was round like the day. Here, too, was food in plenty, and water. Already braves were out hunting and chopping the pines. The women, Singing Beads and Spring Song among them, were stealing from the mice. They would follow the mouse trails in the tall grass until they found the caches of wild beans put away for winter.

When the plan of the camp was determined, Joseph went with Ollokot and Strikes Standing to fish in the river. Grasshoppers sailed through the grass with faintly whickering wings, and they caught a few for bait. At the stream, Joseph drank deep, like a horse, with most of his face plunged into the current. In the shallows, women searched for water-lily roots, which they dug at with their toes until they floated to the surface. Scraped and dried, they would be cooked with the venison the warriors would bring home.

With the help of the grasshoppers, they caught several small trout before dark and started back through the high grass, thanking the insects for their aid. By then the violet glow of evening permeated the air and vapors were rising from the stream. Gnats wafted up into the light of the fading sun, making silver threads in the air. A bat or two hurled themselves through the first shadows.

The hunters were already back. They'd taken enough venison for a feast and were hanging the carcasses up in the trees to keep them from the silver-tipped bears. At their temporary lodge, Spring Song and Singing Beads were preparing supper. The wild beans had been ground to a fine paste, and the fire was crackling. Singing Beads covered it with hot stones. This was their pride. It was wrong of the missionaries to degrade them and their men by urging the braves to join in woman's work. Joseph watched the resolute and rapid way Singing Beads went about her tasks. She knew exactly what she was doing, and she was so full of happy confidence that there was nothing to do but accept the consequences with joy.

Strikes Standing built up the fire. She scooped out a pit for the stones when they were hot, and onto them she placed the trout and the balls of ground beans. All this she covered, and then Spring Song brought water and poured it around the stones until they cracked aloud. Idly, Joseph watched as Strikes Standing uncovered the food. Her large strong hands worked with a steady rhythm, never stopping, never hurrying. He saw the sturdy arch of her neck from the shoulder as she bent over the food, and the long braid of her black hair. All was well. That night he accepted the wisdom of Looking Glass.

The following day the Nez Percé rested at the Big Hole camp. They hunted and fished, played the stick and bean game, dug for camas roots and baked them in pits. Some whites looked down from the mountain slopes in the afternoon. Looking Glass dismissed them as curious settlers. As dusk fell, the Nez Percé gathered around their fires to dance and sing their chants in freedom.

Joseph watched the red sun boiling in the sky. He saw small, fleecy red clouds with golden edges sail across the purpling west. One moment they were stampeding buffalo; the next, they were winged geese. He tried to read a hopeful message in the clouds, but he saw there only flight, endless flight. It was the smell of the wind that bothered him; it was Hattia Tinukin, the death wind. He was not alone in his restlessness. There was something in the air which warned them all to be on guard. It was not the fair place itself, but something menacing in the air, so for lack of another name, they called it Hattia Tinukin.

A council was called which met between the camps. Chiefs and warriors loomed thick and tall, bearing the last of sunset on their shoulders.

"I have nothing to say which has not already been said," Joseph began lamely. "I wish all of you grandfathers to remember the white man, his singing wires, his iron horse with soldiers in its belly, riding its iron paths. Remember the scouts we have all seen in the hills. Why do we feast and celebrate here? What do you say, grandfather?" He turned to Looking Glass.

"We will stay until I say it is time to go," replied Looking Glass.

"Then send out pickets. Let us put scouts on the back trail."

"All are friendly here. We need no scouts who will get into whiskey and shoot our white friends."

"Listen," interjected Five Wounds. "I agree with Joseph, although I have no wife and no children to be endangered by what I feel is coming toward us. Whatever is gained or lost, it is yours."

"This is squaw talk," replied Looking Glass. He stared so directly down his nose that he seemed to be cross-eyed.

Joseph took him by the shoulders. "Grandfather, you are putting us in danger. In the name of the Great Spirit, do you understand what I am saying?" Perhaps behind those unblinking inscrutable eyes dwelt a keen mind, but Joseph could not see past the fierce pride that cared not for caution, cavalry, grizzly bears, the harshness of the trail. Perhaps, indeed, he would welcome another fight to test his strong old bones and muscles. Either he was a fool or he pretended to be.

"If you are dissatisfied with me as head chief, elect another," said Looking Glass. "Joseph, see who stands with you." Many did, in fact—enough to divide a strong camp into two weak ones. That could be no answer, to fall apart fighting among themselves. "Leave, any of you who wish," said Looking Glass. "I stay here with my people until the morning." Even that sounded like a concession, and so the council broke up. Later they would remember it as Piamkin Tinukin—the Council of Death.

Though it was already dark when the council concluded, Joseph and Ollokot toured the camp perimeter. There was little two could do, and they saw and heard nothing suspicious. A large fire burned where Toohoolhoolzote had set down his lodge, and the Dreamer led his braves in moaning chant. Otherwise the camp, the plain, and the mountain fringe were still. Returning to their lodge, the brothers planned to patrol again after eating. But the lodge was warm and lazy, full of love and good cooking smells. Joseph played with his new daughter as he waited for the food. He held her out at arm's length. What a wonder she was—so small, yet so perfect. The face cut like a heart and the dark eyes staring back at him, unblinking, seemed to seek out his deepest thoughts. A wave of hot love surged through him, and with it came defiance. He would compensate for having brought her into this hostile white world. She would not suffer, not while he lived. The baby uttered yells of unbelievable loudness, each one distinct from the last. They were shouts of joy. Laughter sparkled from her eyes.

He would go now. He would take ten warriors and make sure the camp was safe. But when he told Singing Beads, she urged him to stay. "That's Looking Glass's task, not Joseph's. He'll put out warriors if need be."

"You don't know that one," Joseph replied, and he thought of all the brave warriors born to lose their lives bravely. "I must go." But she prevailed upon him to eat first.

The fish was fine—better than the buffalo, or the white man's cattle, which were too sweet and full of fat. It reminded him of the Wallowa. He chewed slowly for the taste, sorting out plans with the grinding of his jaws. In the morning he would leave with his people. Whatever Looking Glass said, he would leave and head north. Meanwhile, perhaps one night of rest and food might help them on the trek. He gave a bit of fish to the old dog, who sat as always beside him at the fire. The dog choked it down, the fish never touching his teeth. Then he resumed his position, grinning with ferocious pleasure. His small eyes blinked in the smoke which coiled like phantom snakes toward the ridgepoles.

I must go, Joseph thought. But the food and the warmth held him. Through glazed eyes, he watched Singing Beads rise as silent and graceful as the smoke. She was preparing the lodge for sleep—but he must not be seduced. How beautiful she was. How solemnly she compelled him with those deep black eyes under wide brow—eyes more peaceful than the mountain springs. "I love you like the summer sky," he said in his mind. "I love the way you sing, warm and deep in your throat. I love Spring Song because she is like you, a graceful young willow in the breeze; and Strikes Standing, for she is an oak tree which will not bend or break. I love my baby, nursing at its finger, fretting when no milk will come." He couldn't help laughing at the baby's efforts; and Singing Beads laughed, too, as they had laughed together so often in the Wallowa. But the baby knitted its brows together with a solemn heaviness of face as if it were trying to comprehend want and something that approached pain. In those offended eyes was a burden he must learn to bear.

He loved them all. They looked so peaceful, it was a joy to watch them from silence. As long as they were together, and Ollokot stood by him, the world was not all darkness.

"Come sleep," Singing Beads urged him.

"I will, I will soon," he replied.

And he did lie down beside her so that she would feel reassured and would sleep. Unconsciously he rubbed pine needles between his fingers. Immediately the forest fragrance perfumed the lodge. "I could sleep for a while and then go outside. That would do as well." The odor of the pine and his wife's gentle breathing called him down to slumber, and then a fly, a simple black fly, alighted on his wife's shoulder. It turned a curious half circle, exploring, and it was for him an abrupt reminder of mortality, of the death and decay he had noticed on the wind.

Silently he arose. No one stirred. Ollokot was asleep, and there seemed no reason to disturb him. Plenty of warriors were still abroad, gambling, singing, and dancing around the glow of fires. These were the veterans, their faces burnished bright as bronze in the flames. They were remembering forgotten times. The exhorter, Culculhensah, danced near the embers like an old moth. He hummed a chant, saying the words softly. It was an ancient song about one who was doomed and knew it, who had accepted that doom as he would accept the rising of the sun. Joseph had forgotten many of the words, though the rhythm was as his own heartbeat. The fire, too, was beautiful. He gazed at it long with unblinking eyes, imagining what it would be like to stare thus at the sun.

In the end, Joseph went alone on his patrol. Rabbits bounded quietly on either side. Crickets screamed, falling silent as he passed. The rustle of grass behind him brought him up short. He whirled to face a slight figure, black against the night.

"Spring Song," he whispered.

"You mustn't guard the camp all alone," she said.

"Quiet, then."

They walked by the whispering river. How beautiful was the untouched night. Then a cry like a bugle caught them short, until Joseph realized it was one of the wild young squaws out tempting her lover to a desperate hide-and-seek in the dark. Even such unwitting sentinels were good to have. The cry came again, farther now, and it ended in laughter. Joseph and his daughter continued their stealthy sweep around the camp. The crickets made no sound. Even the river gave no sound of motion. All listened. For ghostly laughter on the air, for the crack of a rifle bolt, the stumbling of a horse, its rider's curse? There was only the murmur of the night wind peeling back the leaves, separating the clouds to let the starlight down. It fell on the Big Hole like a silver rain of arrows let fly by the warriors of old. Toward the north, Spring Song pointed out the hunter star with a pack on his back, red now, a drop of blood over the pines. Dawn would come early, and Joseph had learned nothing. If a dozen braves had accompanied him, he might have learned no more. So they started back toward the glow-worm flicker of the Nez Percé camp.

The great "V" of tipis was silent. The village slept. No one stirred at his arrival. Singing Beads slept as he had left her, like a bird, with one arm over her face. He envied the ease of her slumber, which seemed to enfold her without concern for the day to come. Even when sleep finally took him, he was not visited by the butterfly, giver of refreshing dreams. He became a horse in a vast meadow enclosed by split-rail fences. He was frisky and wild, and he finally jumped the rails. Those who watched were terrified. They screamed, taking after him with lances and knives. This dream gave way to a nightmare in which he dreamed a dream within a dream of something that he couldn't name. From this he awakened deadly cold. A finger of moonlight touched the dog at the tipi entrance. He stirred in shallow sleep. Then he stood up, ears pricked, listening for a sound that never came. He slept again before his master slept.

Joseph felt the pulsebeat in his forehead. What had awakened him then? There was a hollow, empty feeling inside him that knew before he knew that the safe buffalo shield of the night was even then beginning to lift. The moonlight was gone, but there was enough light for him to see that fog filled the Big Hole. The katydids were still. Soon the sun would overflow the prairie.

Now the dog lay awake, tail stirring, looking at Joseph with expectant eyes as if he were about to reveal the secrets of the future. Singing Beads's closed lids were like two tiny dark wings upon her cheeks. Asleep, she was still a young girl. Silently he stroked her cheek. His heart filled with love and pity. No sound came from the other lodges. Even the babies were silent as though smothered at their mothers' breasts. Presently he must wake them, for he was determined to press on north in spite of Looking Glass. His own baby awakened and yawned at him with a mouth red and toothless as a turtle. Seeing his eyes, it smiled widely and dribbled with a generous display of gums. "Little one," he whispered, "you be my sun caller today. Tell them how hungry you are." Then he went to the entrance of the lodge and sucked at the morning air. No one was abroad. His poor weary people . . . Soon they must be up and moving. He would press them hard from now on. It was the only safe way.

The sun already was gilding the highest treetops. A golden bird perched above his head, and in the stillness he could hear the seeds cracking in its beak. Then Ollokot pushed up beside him, his lids still heavy with sleep. When the baby began to announce its hunger and the new day's arrival, they turned back inside. Strikes Standing stirred the embers into a glow. Each day starts the same, Joseph thought. Then, with the abrupt shock of a blow struck at the base of his skull, there rang out a single rifle shot. After an instant of silence a volley of shots sounded, followed by anguished shouting. More shots, ragged but constant now. A bullet splintered through the lodgepoles overhead.

Big man that he was, Joseph found his feet like a cat. The look of uncomprehending wonder was gone from his face. He knew. Ollokot was beside him as he burst outside. A bugle uttered its piercing stammer, ta-ta-tata-tatta-ta, and its call conjured up a swarm of birds from the thickets near the river.

The mist-shrouded meadow was filled now with shouting strangers. They roared as they came, a serious, deep roar. Those fuzzy boys in blue shirts had a wild indignant look on their faces as though it was themselves and not the Nez Percé who were being attacked without warning or mercy.

The force which began the Battle of the Big Hole consisted of sixteen officers and 146 men and it included the garrison from Fort Fizzle. Attached to this Seventh Infantry were forty-five volunteers from Stevensville, who had come along despite their non-aggression pact with the Nez Percé. In command was Colonel John Gibbon, known to the Indians as The One Who Limps. He did not believe in taking Indian prisoners. Before they moved up to the attack, he told his troops to spare no one, man, woman, or child, so long as their skin was red.

Toward dawn, the skirmish line had drawn closer through the willow-wooded bottom land near the creek. There had been no alarm until an old warrior, Natalekin, rode unknowing from his tipi. His eyes were poor and he wished a private bath, for the children made fun of his wrinkled stiffness in and out of the water. Figures moving toward him had looked unreal and ghostly in the early mist, and he had leaned forward to make them out just as the first shot had taken his life. From that moment, the attack had moved quickly. The soldiers had plunged through the shallow stream and up the bank, firing on the first Indians who burst from their tipis. Into the confusion of screaming women, dogs, babies, they rushed—shooting, stabbing, clubbing their way, rolling up the two wings of the Indian camp which White Bird and Looking Glass occupied.

It was into this approaching chaos that Joseph stepped, into a confusion of screams and gunpowder and smoky haze lit by horrors. The blue figures moved more slowly now, staggering drunkenly out of the curling vapor. Pahka Pahtanhank, Five Fogs, eldest son of Hahtalekin, was the first to rally. Clad in his white King George blanket and armed only with a bow and arrows, for he was no warrior, he walked into the fire of the advancing enemy, an example to them all, until he fell.

Joseph rallied the braves around him. The first shock was over. It no longer even seemed strange, for he had experienced it all before in his forebodings. A circle of defense began to form before his lodge. "Shoot low! Shoot low!" he directed them. "Waste no bullets. We must hold here." Children clung to him, aware of his strength, sensing perhaps that he would not die that day, and the warriors who responded to his call fought with the calmness of those who had been forced into a desperate game which must be won.

In the shattered stillness of that summer morning, the battle became a strange and dream-like affair. At times, curling mist and smoke were the only target, until the soldiers burst through, shouting, receiving their measure of pain and death. Joseph cautioned his braves to shoot slowly. Sometimes he found himself firing at clusters, but he knew he shouldn't do that, he couldn't afford the ammunition. "Take aim from the shoulder," he told them. The soldiers came on, firing from the hip, often as not with their eyes shut. They had bullets to waste.

On the left, Lieutenant Bradley was killed, and his leaderless men turned to burning the camp. The buffalo skins were wet with mist and refused to ignite. Furiously they persisted, giving White Bird time to gather his scattered braves. "Why are we retreating?" he screamed like an eagle. "Since the world was made, brave men fight for their women and children. Fight!" The soldiers began to pull back. Some were surounded. In desperation they began digging in on the camp's fringe.

With the tide turned, Joseph's heart was with his people. It was still too dangerous for stripping and moving the lodges. The most he could do was help women and children to the safety of the river bank. Singing Beads had been grazed across the back of her hand. She seemed stunned, and Spring Song guided her. Joseph followed with the baby in his arms. He looked for Strikes Standing to help the wounded, but could not find her. Returning, he found an old squaw, tiny, confused as a gray owl in sudden light, standing amid the whine of bullets. He pulled her to shelter. Turning back to the camp, he met a warrior who dragged himself along on his elbows, slowly and stiffly. His lips pouted, the frozen look of a child who refuses something repulsive. "Red Moccasin Tops!"

His lips moved soundlessly as Joseph tried to help him. He'd been shot through the throat and the trail behind him was red. Again came the crimson bubbling and his lips opened and closed, opened and closed until he died.

Crouching down, Joseph picked him up and slung him over his shoulder like a dead stag. He felt the wounded man's life oozing down his legs as he staggered under the burden. For all the blood he had lost, the warrior seemed heavier, heavy as a stone, as a mountain. Behind the river bank, Joseph let down his burden softly, though it could not matter to the warrior now. Then he, too, lay down briefly himself, streaming sweat and panting, not from weariness but from the terrible rage that was battle's aftermath. In a moment he rose, for there were others who needed him.

By late afternoon the Nez Percé had regained their camp. The troops were withdrawing with their wounded. Among them was Colonel Gibbon himself, who would be known henceforth as He Who Limps Twice. They had thrown the rifles of their dead into the river. In pursuit, the braves had captured and overturned the howitzer and had closed about the soldiers, who held a wooded slope in desperate defense. A sniping duel commenced at long range. Among their weapons the Nez Percé had telescopic hunting rifles equipped with exploding bullets. The soldiers dared not move. The Indians could not attack them over open ground, yet victory had been snatched from defeat—a ghastly victory made horribly clear as they retook lodge after lodge and discovered their mutilated dead: women and young girls, and babies with their heads broken. Relatives gashed their arms with grief and blackened their faces in mourning, and a dreadful anger pervaded the camp. The grim and throbbing hatred led to a reckless assault on the soldiers which failed. Another, better planned, almost succeeded, until the wind shifted and turned the fire that the Indians had set in the thick brush against themselves.

Dusk found them still embattled. Grief rose slowly in the night. Joseph had been lucky. Singing Beads and her children lived. Ollokot returned from the fighting without a scratch. Even his dog had come through unscathed. But when he returned to the lodge with his family, they found Strike Standing. A trooper lay dead in the entrance and behind him Strikes Standing knelt by the smoldering fire. She knelt as she had knelt so many mornings and evenings, keeper of the flame in his lodge. Her own fire was out, carried away by a musket ball that had entered her face and plowed out the back of her head. She must have died instantly, and yet some will power beyond death kept her at her post.

Seeing her, Singing Beads put her hand across her mouth as a gag. Joseph put his arm around his young wife. Only by the shaking of her body could he tell that she was crying, for she made no sound. He was silent, too, though he could feel the twisting of his facial muscles into the ugliness of grief. "I must be as loyal as she," he thought. "I must bury her now, though I am weary. I must bury her deep, so that no wolf, no bear, no Bannock brave will disturb her rest." And this he did, alone, that night.

When he returned, Singing Beads sat where Strikes Standing had been. The fire glowed. The dead trooper was gone. In his place was Ollokot's wife, alive, but wounded in the side at close range. She looked as though she'd been clawed by wolves. Ollokot pleaded with her to live. Perhaps she heard him. At least she did not die that night. Ollokot tried to make her eat. The others ate and spoke of tomorrow.

"Tomorrow we will finish them," Ollokot promised.

"Tomorrow we must flee from this place," said Joseph, "before One-Armed Howard comes."

"Perhaps that is better," Ollokot agreed. "We have lost many good warriors." Wahlitits had died in the first charge. His wife, already wounded, had seized his rifle and killed one advancing trooper before she herself was killed.

"He saw his death coming," Joseph said. Perhaps it even was deserved, as he had much to do with starting the trouble. Red Moccasin Tops, too, had died by the river bank where Joseph had laid him down. He was buried now under the bank in a shallow grave. That too had been a reckoning. Ollokot said that Rainbow had fallen. His Wyakin had promised him he would never die in a battle fought after sunrise, but Five Wounds had found his body in the willows. In despair, he had concluded that Rainbow must have died before the first light, perhaps without ever firing a shot. "My brother is no more, and I shall follow him," Five Wounds had lamented, and those who heard him bowed their heads, for they knew what he intended.

To the whites who saw his death charge, it must have seemed as though an Indian had gone mad. Five Wounds had lunged straight through the open. The first volley caught him as he came on, drove through him, but did not halt him for a moment. A thicket barred his way, a six-foot ledge of rock, but he was transformed in his last strength. He became a weapon hurled toward the cowering soldiers. They fired again as he drove on, clawing up the rock. He received a third and a fourth volley before he went down, and then his gun was raised to his shoulder, though his body was shattered and bathed in blood. Surely by then the troopers knew what manner of men they fought. Surely, as they cowered in the dark waiting for the dawn, they were afraid. They had already lost twice the number of fighting men as the Nez Percé. That was their defeat; but the women and children on the field who breathed no more were the Nez Percé tragedy.

At first light on the second day of the Big Hole battle, Joseph stood in the ashes. The catastrophe of yesterday's misty dawn had cut into his heart. He would never dislodge it. He wanted to call out to the forsaking gods and tell them this was wrong. But long ago he had lost faith in the Indian gods, and the white man's God was a savage hater of all men. Quietly he whispered his sorrow chant. Minor griefs might be shouted, but for such tragedy there was only silence.

The fighting went on sporadically. Both sides were hurt too badly for an attack, and with the rising sun the blood of the day before began to exude a sweet and vomitous odor. Nearby lay a dead pony, scaled with flies. A buzzard approached it, walking stiffly, turning its old scalped head back over its shoulder to see if Joseph meant to compete for its prize. Joseph ran at it, waving his arms. The bird began its lumbering, wing-beating run, and finally gained the air. It was foolish to blame the birds for their impatience. Beside the dead pony Joseph stopped, breathing hard. Fool, to run after birds. He needed his strength for the trail. Then he saw the woman's body. She lay beside the pony, her arm broken and her hand shattered. She must have been protecting her face from the destroying gun fired at arm's length. There, too, was a child, wounded but somehow alive. It managed to rock toward him on legs still half bowed as if not entirely straightened from the womb. It tried to cry, but had no strength, and its mouth pulled at the air like that of a salmon cast on the bank. He picked the child up. "We'll find you a mother," he told it. Perhaps Singing Beads for now, he thought, as he started back toward camp. The child coughed against his shoulder and he crooned to it a half-forgotten song. In all this death he had saved a life. But before he arrived at the tipi, he knew it had ceased to be a child at all. It was simply another corpse to be buried. This task he performed quickly, while from the woods came the repeated cry of a crippled owl. He thought it was that at first, then he realized it was a trooper in pain, crying without shame. To what lengths these white men went to bring down suffering on everyone, even themselves. No matter how much longer he lived—until he perished in a battle yet unnamed, or until age dimmed his visions

—these pictures seen at the Big Hole would remain seared into his eyes, the way a brilliant light will leave a terrible reversed image of itself when the eyes are closed.

Seventy-five Indians were buried that morning, mostly in shallow graves in the river bank. Among these, only twelve were good warriors. The process was undertaken with general grief, and fury—fury at the white settlers of Montana who had betrayed their trust, fury at life, and at Looking Glass. More than one survivor shot out his finger toward the old chief in a gesture meaning, "I could kill you and not be satisfied doing it." Looking Glass absorbed it all in silence. He retained a certain majesty, like an old tree that has been struck by lightning but still stands. With his own hands he buried his daughter, and some said it was the only time in his life that he had cried.

From behind rock rifle pits, the Nez Percé sniped at the troopers. Some counseled attack and the taking of scalps in revenge. Then from the dead was extracted a living white volunteer from Stevensville. Joseph recognized the little storekeeper with the expensive bullets. He'd been feigning death among the honest dead, and now they demanded information from him. He held nothing back. General Howard and Virginia City volunteers were expected at any time to finish the Indians off. A grief-stricken squaw slapped at him. The prisoner kicked back, and then the warriors were upon him. When they withdrew, his body was torn as though by grizzlies. If they find him, they will call us savages, thought Joseph. But he could not blame them. His own hand had gone to the knife at his belt when the man had kicked out. Only at the last had he restrained himself.

Then Joseph called together all those who were not wounded or guarding the camp. "We must go toward the Land of the Old Lady," he told them. "Now, before the coming of One-Armed Howard. You must put your wounded on travois and leave this place. We are safe only in flight." He spoke above the regular chuck-chuck of the gravedigging. He told them what they must do, and the hearts of the Nez Percé returned to him. "Poker Joe will be our trail-finder. He knows the land of the buffalo. I will look after the women and children, and Ollokot will come last. He will tell us what One-Armed Howard is doing."

The last dirt was clawed down from the river bank onto the dead, and the travois, black and clotted with old death, were loaded again with the wounded and dying. It was the practice of some tribes to leave the old and sick behind for the wolves. This was never so with the Nez Percé, and Joseph said to them now: "Who has ever heard of a wounded Indian recovering while in the hands of white men?" By noon the column was under way. Poker Joe rode ahead, marking the trail. Joseph and White Bird led the families, while sporadic fighting sputtered in the Big Hole. Ollokot commanded the warriors there, though he had broken off to take leave of his wounded wife. She had lain on her side on the travois. Her eyes were wide open like those of a hurt rabbit and they glittered with pain. "You are good and strong," Ollokot told her. "You are for me the only one." He commanded her to live. Breathing harshly through her teeth, she made her husband a promise that Joseph knew it would be hard for her to keep.

The Nez Percé moved along the western edge of the timbered mountains, heading at first southward where the valley on the east was wide. Here there could be no surprises. Ahead was the Bloody Dick Creek trail and the valley of Horse Prairie Creek. Behind them, little brown birds pecked the stained sand of the Big Hole and buzzards tilted, swooped, and turned in lazy flight. Joseph's eyes went up now and again to follow their courses across the blue. The sight touched him with doubt and produced images of ragged bones and decaying flesh. High in the mountains were the eagles, who never descended to this torn and warring plain.

They marched all that day into Looking Glass's beloved buffalo prairies. On either side, the white-tailed barkers of the mountain meadows watched them. These were the fat, potbellied ground squirrels that the white men called prairie dogs. Sun worshippers, curious beyond caution, they watched the Indians pass by, giving their high "Yek-yek-yek" of warning only when a horse strayed too close. More distant were the pronghorn sheep. Almost too fast to be hunted, they would raise their white rump patches in a heliographic flash of warning whenever a brave rode close. Of the buffalo, nothing was to be seen beyond the dry manure of past years.

"They are like us," Joseph thought. "Driven from

their homes. Only the cattle have hope in the long run, and cattle are without courage or dignity."

The mountains forced them south all day. There was no chilly warning of the passing year. A smoky haze hung over the land and crows cried dismally from afar. It was summer still, with warmth and color undiminished. Winter would come quickly as they turned north. Hundreds of miles still separated them from the safety of Canada, harsh safety at best if they arrived in the winter. He must get them there quickly, all of them. He checked his horse, as the people slogged by. Their faces were masks of anger, fear, and torment. Without order they crossed the plain, and their expressions were all the same. Dust rose around them, and he felt himself the father of every one that passed. They were all his to care for, no matter what their age.

VIII
The Long Retreat

The Nez Percé camped at a place called The Willows. Refugees in a world of hostile whites, they posted guards. Joseph prowled without sleep until dawn, when he got them moving again. He walked beside his daughter Spring Song, resting his pony and wondering how long they could keep up such a pace. The night and the day before, and the day before that had gone by in broken shards of space and time, fused only by fear and doubt and the struggle to suppress hunger.

No longer was an effort made to appease the settlers. When they needed ponies, the braves took them without payment. On the Horse Prairie, a skirmish developed over stock. Some ranchers were killed. From there they moved down Cruikshank Canyon toward a stockade at the Lemhi River. Shoshonis rode out to urge them away from the whites. They wanted no trouble, and neither did Joseph, though some of the warriors menaced the stockade, riding around it on horseback. No shots were fired.

Although Ollokot had not returned, Joseph knew they were again being followed. He had seen the Bannocks, usually a score or more, keeping at a safe distance, but always within view. Bannocks, Shoshonis, all the tribes seemed against them, ready to have them expelled or hunted down.

That evening, as camp was being made, Ollokot returned with his braves. They had waited near the Big Hole battlefield until Howard had come, guided by Buffalo Horn and his Bannocks. Blood-blackened iron tomahawks hung from their hands as they explored the battlefield for life or death. Like wolves on a scent, the Bannocks worked back and forth over the killing ground until the graves of the Nez Percé were found. Then, with the troopers standing by, they had disenterred, robbed, and mutilated the festering dead.

"They spared no one?" Joseph asked.

"No one. Only the babies too young for hair were not scalped."

"Strikes Standing?"

"Brother, I was far away. I didn't see everything."

"One day we will go back and bury them again," Joseph said.

"One day."

Both knew it would never happen.

"None must be left behind, not even those who die," Joseph said.

"Is my wife . . ." Ollokot began.

"She lives. Come."

Joseph had unhitched the travois from the pack horse, but he had dared not move the girl from it, as though the leather thongs that bound her were all that kept her life from escaping. She moved her large dark eyes toward Ollokot as he knelt beside her. They alone seemed alive, black, bright as polished silver under thick lashes, and full of torment. He held her hand. "You will be better soon," he said, and nothing more.

The brothers withdrew. "Her hand was hot," Ollokot said. "I thought it would be cold. She is hurt worse than the grizzly we shot. Still she lives. How can she live, hurt that way?"

"She lives for you."

"I know," Ollokot said. "How can I tell her to die?" For a moment his face gave way, torn by suffering as if sorrow had twisted it into a mask of grotesque pain. Abruptly he turned away.

There were times to be alone. This was one of them, and so Joseph left him. What consolation could he give? On the night air, heavy with the scent of pine, he could smell death.

Still she lived throughout the night, and throughout the hard trek of the following day, which led to the wide grassy plain known as the Camas Meadows. Here clear streams ran down from the foothills of sage and aspen, which were already tinted with autumn. Like the Big Hole, it had long been a favorite rendezvous of the hunters.

Toward dawn, mist rose from the stream and spider webs were beaded with dew. The wounded girl lay awake with a great terror in her eyes. She opened and closed her mouth like a throttled bird, but, though Ollokot leaned close, he heard no words. "Please die," he whispered. "Go where there is peace."

Now she will die, Joseph thought. He had been wrong before, but not this time. With the first tint of eastern light, her face composed itself. Her breathing stopped.

Ollokot turned to his brother. He, too, looked as though he had died a violent death.

"The Bannocks must never have her," he whispered.

"Come, let us bury her together. There is a place."

They carried her up a rocky gorge amid sharp lava outcroppings, and there, in a deep rocky draw, they buried her in her blanket. No bird called. No dog howled.

"Now she has peace," Joseph said. "May her spirit roam happy in the land of the dead." This was a formula which he had long since ceased to believe.

They covered the grave with brush and then returned to camp. Joseph roused the people for departure, but they were again delayed by another burial. Gray Eagle, an old man from White Bird's band, had been wounded at the Big Hole. After muttering his ghost song for two days and two nights, he had finally expired as much from exhaustion and age as from his wound. His entire family had been slain at the battle except one daughter, White Feather, who had been shot in the shoulder and clubbed in the mouth with a rifle butt. She was not yet strong enough to bury her father alone. She had no one to help her and no horse to carry him. Rather than abandon the body to the ravages of the pursuing Bannocks, she had elected to stay with her father.

"They will kill and scalp you, too," Joseph told her. "Will you come with us if we bury him?" She nodded, scarcely able to speak through her ruined mouth. He went with her back to the gulch and buried the old man under rubble and branches with his rusty cap and ball pistol beside him.

"Now will you come, poor Imwholise?" he asked her, calling her "Broken Tooth" out of sympathy. Again she nodded, and he was glad she did not know the Bannocks as well as he did. He felt sure they would sniff out this grave, and that of Ollokot's wife, too. That was the Bannock way. But there was nothing more he could do for the dead. His heart must be with those who lived.

Joseph's breath smoked in the golden light as he gave the order to move north. Poker Joe took the point, as usual. Looking Glass glowered behind. Ollokot and White Bird guarded the flanks, and particularly the pony herd. The Bannock tribesmen were after the stock. They had already driven off several head. Some Crow braves had joined these raiders, though in years past the Nez Percé had aided the Crow against their mortal foe, the Sioux. *And now we go to join our enemy in Canada,* Joseph thought as he watched the passing column. *If he could be as the eagle, if he could look down on all this from above—would he laugh, or cry, or would he tilt his wings and soar away, heedless of the stretching dust of the Nez Percé trail, the hilltops seeded with Bannock watchers, and One-Armed Howard jolting behind with his Bible and his troopers?* Howard would have no women and children, no wounded to slow him down. But this was not the life for a white man. They would be feeling it, too; and yet they would not stop until the Nez Percé were taken or were in Canada. Joseph seemed to see the bare telegraph poles lifting their spider threads of wire, singing the white man's war songs. He seemed to see the double glinting iron rails. Somewhere a war chief called Sheridan, about whom he had heard, sat with a map, looking down on the world as only the eagle could, and moving his men. "If I could see such a map," thought Joseph, "we would be safe. If I could only see where this Wind River Post is." He had word that Washakie's band of Shoshoni, one hundred fresh braves, had been martialed there against them—Washakie in his gray blouse, fat, good-natured, accepting the white man's ways along with his silken guidon.

Joseph had no map and would have found it unintelligible if he had one. Nor could he rise like the eagle. But even in the black of night, blindfolded, he would have known north as surely as a compass feels that pull, and north he drove his people to their limits, because it was their only hope. Most went fearfully through the strange land. All were hungry and full of hate for those whites and Indians who had betrayed them. Some few wished to make an end to flight. Better to stand and fight and die, they protested. But these were few, mostly young braves of Toohoolhoolzote's band, and the chiefs were against them. That afternoon the braves rode off looking for trouble.

At the ranches of Daniel Winters and W. L. Montague, they found it. Four farmers were killed, but a haying party escaped into the woods. Talking Possum, who led this band, found breech-loading carbines in both ranch houses, and took them. Then they broke up their muzzle loaders on the sturdy furniture. They also discovered liquor. More joined in the raiding the following day. Joseph could hold them back no more, though he admonished them. "We make no war on women or children. We take no scalps." In this alone, they heeded him. Following Stephenson's Canyon to the valley of the Lemhi River, they came upon a resting mule train of eight covered wagons, thirty mules, three drivers, and four passengers. The cargo consisted of groceries, ammunition, and ten barrels of whiskey bound for Salmon City. Poker Joe, who had gone along to study the trail, held Talking Possum back at first. "Don't shoot. We fight only soldiers." But in the end the whiskey had a louder voice. The drivers, all Chinese, got away. The white passengers were not so fortunate. Talking Possum, a knee-walking drunk by this time, began to blacksnake-whip Daniel Coombs. He didn't have the strength to do real damage, but it got things started. A gun went off, then several. The white men died. His face bloated with drink, Talking Possum drew out his scalping knife. Five Snows, one of Joseph's braves, opposed him. They shot it out amid the ruins of the smoldering mule train. Talking Possum fired wildly and often; Five Snows placed one careful shot in the other's abdomen and it was finished, all but the painful dying. That took three days, after which Talking Possum was left behind, unmourned and unburied, for the Bannocks.

Sometime later, sixteen braves of Joseph's band were out cutting telegraph wires. South of Pleasant Valley they discovered the Hole in the Rock stage depot, cut all the wires there, destroyed the grain at the station, and disrupted the stage. A holiday party, complete with picnic baskets and parasols, cowered nearby. They looked harmless enough, and the braves left them. No great harm was done, and yet, as Joseph well knew, it was one more pebble cast into the rippling lake of wild rumor. It would swell the tales of savages sprung from the wilderness to scalp and mutilate. It would further harden the hearts of those who dwelt in the lands through which they must pass. Better that they turn their pent-up furies upon the real enemy than on picnickers and mule-skinners. This decision was reinforced by the return to camp of two scouts who had seen Howard's dust column approaching the Camas Meadows. Back there at the Meadows, on familiar ground, was where they must strike. An old warrior wounded at the Big Hole had had a vision of the Nez Percé successfully driving off the troopers' horses. This vision confirmed the council.

Ollokot offered to lead the raid. Fearing that his brother's grief for his wife might make him reckless, Joseph said: "Brother, you must guard the camp this time. I have heard that Washakie and his braves are near."

"My place is with the warriors," Ollokot insisted.

"Since your wife died . . ." Joseph began.

"Do not speak of it. Brother, I do not seek death, if you think that. I love life still."

"Then you will guard the camp, if you are my brother," Joseph said. "Looking Glass has asked for a place among the warriors." This was true. Whether the old chief sought redemption or merely honorable death, Joseph could not tell. He had received from Looking Glass only a slow smile, quiet and terrible. It would be well to have him with the war party, and, as he was now, it would be no great loss should he fall.

The moon was rising as the war party set out. Except for twenty-five who remained on guard with White Bird, every healthy brave rode that night from the camp at Shotgun Creek back to the Camas Meadow, where Ollokot's wife lay buried. Occasional clouds obscured the moon. Rain showers, together with the imminence of attack, kept the braves alert. The grass grew thicker as they proceeded down the narrowing valley and it muffled the sound of hoofs. They moved slowly, waiting for the moon to set behind the mountains. No Bannock scout or trooper challenged their approach or noted where they dismounted in the deep shadow of the forest fringe.

As they waited for the moon to vanish, the party was divided into those who would creep into the sleeping camp and cut loose the horses, and those who would form a firing line once the theft was discovered. Joseph led the advance party. Before they reached the camp, the darkness was complete. A horse stirred restlessly, and the sound guided them above the murmur of the stream. No sentinel challenged them. Then the forms of the tethered horses loomed up. For some time they worked silently, cutting thongs, creeping slowly through the herd. Suddenly, without the slightest warning, a solitary shot cracked out. Otskai, a young brave with Looking Glass's band, had fired from sheer excitement. His finger had tightened on the trigger, and with that report the surprise was over. The Indian line tore in and over the waking camp. Above the yelling, neighing confusion, one great voice thundered. It was Looking Glass, urging on his braves as though he would take a blunder and turn it into a triumph. Now the darkness hindered them all. There were no targets, only sounds to shoot at. They heard the splash of Callaway's startled volunteers as they stampeded into the creek. Even with eyes grown accustomed to the night, it was hard to distinguish a brave from a trooper naked but for his long red underwear. Then, to compound the uncertainty, came the horses. Some two hundred had been cut free, and with a crash of hoofs, they were off. Joseph was knocked to the ground. He saw hoofs like wings flying about him, and the flash of white underbellies. Struggling sideways, he managed to swing himself to the back of a frightened animal. There were other straddling figures about him, and the tide of loosed mounts thundered past the line of firing braves and into the quiet before dawn. For some time they rode hard, and then they gradually slowed down. The beasts trotted on stiff legs.

It wasn't until the first real light, when Looking Glass and the other braves overtook them with their ponies, that the truth dawned. Joseph noticed it first in his own mount, then in his companion's. He hadn't been riding a cavalry horse at all, but a pack mule. They were all pack mules. In the darkness, they'd stolen the wrong herd. It wasn't a mistake they could correct, now that it was daylight and the troopers were alerted. In fact, they hadn't gone many miles before the horses they'd wanted were after them.

"Don't worry. You have only cavalry men against you," Joseph shouted to his disappointed men, now mounted on their own ponies. He was right. Mounted, the Nez Percé brave was more than a match for a trooper—twisting, spinning, as hard to hit as a bird in flight. The shooting was at long range, with the Indians always withdrawing, protecting what they had seized. Within an hour, however, the fight slowed, and Joseph took up a position in the lava hillocks seven miles from the Camas Meadows. Here among the lava knobs grew sagebrush and aspen, all aflame with autumn. The Indians held, giving time for the herd to escape. At first they sniped at long distance. Then, with Looking Glass and Joseph urging them on, they turned the Army's flank. The troopers pulled back. Casualties were few. Bernard Brooks, a trumpeter, was shot from his horse. The horse stood by him as Brooks tried to pull himself up by the stirrup strap. It was a last effort, for he fell to the ground dead, the only man killed outright in the lava-bed fight. Throughout the long-range duel that followed, the horse stood still like a white-marble statue by his fallen master.

"If we had taken that horse and all the others like him, we would be free now," Joseph pondered. He wanted to capture the animal, for it would be at least a token of success. But before the Nez Percé could drive the troopers from the last two knolls of lava and sage,

General Howard was sighted, coming up with the whole command. The Nez Percé had to give way, richer by one hundred and fifty pack animals and a few superficial wounds. They had lost the chance of taking their pursuers by surprise. That chance would not come again.

White Bird and Ollokot had the tribe in motion when the warriors returned. Joseph embraced his brother. "You do my job as well as I," he said.

"And you, brother . . . If only you knew a horse when you saw him."

Yet they were for a moment two happy leaders. Together, they were more than that; they were indomitable.

"Grandfather, does your wound not hurt?"

Joseph put his hand to his forehead and felt a stickiness there: a stray bullet in the fight? The glancing blow of a horse's hoof? He did not know, and yet it burned all day as they rode north. Again there would be days and nights without food or sleep, as they raced One-Armed Howard and the cooling sun toward the north.

IX
The Yellowstone

With Poker Joe still acting as their guide, they plunged into the Yellowstone country in the last week of August—eight hundred Nez Percé and two thousand horses, with each lodge driving its own herd. Many horses were limping. Their route had begun to swing from the north to a more easterly course, which disturbed Joseph, particularly when Poker Joe admitted he only knew the country second-hand. Luckily, they came upon the fire of John Shivley, a solitary camper who had never heard of the Nez Percé war. He was a prospector, not a guide, he told them, and with arms folded, he challenged them to blow out his brains. A couple of braves were willing to oblige, but in the end Shivley decided he would lead them to the Crow country after all. This he did for the better part of two weeks. Once the route was fixed, they let him escape.

It was splendid, untamed country, reminding Joseph of the Wallowa. The air was so clear he could follow an eagle up and up into the bottomless depths of the sky. Ahead rose the mountains, and on either side of the trail the forests were dashed with a tawny fierceness, each tree seeming to draw down the burnished autumn sun. The fawns, seen now and then through the forest growth, were losing their spots. The season was passing too fast and the great spongy mountain meadows, some with deep quagmires where the streams came down, were almost impossible for the horses. Going was tediously slow.

On the cold mornings, the hot geyser pools were welcome. Some of the older members of the tribe thought they had found paradise. Joseph had trouble moving them along. "The white man's hell must be below there." Perhaps that bothered them, as did the mists which rose like spirits of the dead. In any case, they surrendered the pools for the trail.

Joseph rode up and down the column looking for stragglers. Spring Song, riding beside her father, was excited about the country.

"Is this the way the Land of the Old Lady will be?" she asked.

"I don't know," he told her. "It may be icy and cold with the wind blowing always." He had heard such things. However it turned out, it would not be home, not ever for him and for many of the older ones. Perhaps for Spring Song and his baby, and this became his hope—to make a home for them. A few more weeks and that would be assured. He did not worry for Spring Song. The way she held her head when she walked had the best of the Nez Percé past in it. They would never capture or tame his daughter.

Later that day, nine prisoners were taken, tourists from Radersburg. They included George Cowan, a truculent man with a bullish manner toward Indians; his young wife Emma; and her brother and sister, Frank and Ida Carpenter. Ida was only thirteen. The remainder of the group were hunters. Looking Glass was the first chief to interview them. He did not want to leave spies behind as had happened at the Big Hole, and with his braves he weighed the virtues of killing the tourists. Scalps were easier to pack. In the end, he sent them along to Poker Joe, who spoke with the whites in English, hoping for information. They knew nothing of Howard; they were simply visiting the new Yellowstone Park. That was clear from the start. Disappointed, Poker Joe traded them lame horses for their good ones. Warriors took possession of a violin and a guitar. While the braves were momentarily distracted by the agonized sounds extracted from these instruments, two of the hunters, A. J. Arnold and William Dingee, made a dash for the thick forest. Shots were fired after them, but no pursuit was undertaken. This made things harder for the seven prisoners who remained, particularly George Cowan, who had been overbearing from the start. Braves harassed them beyond Poker Joe's control, and finally a shot was fired. Cowan fell from his horse. There on the trail, with his wife screaming as they dragged her away, Cowan was beaten and left for dead. Somehow he managed to crawl into the brush and was rescued two days later by the first detail of Howard's scouts.

For the safety of the remaining prisoners, the group was broken up for the night. Frank Carpenter and his sisters were delivered to Joseph. It was the first he had heard of the episode.

"Do not be afraid," he told them, though he knew they did not understand his speech. "You are with Joseph." The white man glared at him from behind enlarging spectacles which gave back the same mindless hatred Joseph had observed in other white man's eyes. The man's hands opened and shut beneath fringed cuffs.

Joseph showed the pair a place at the campfire. It was already cold, and he returned to offer them hot broth from his family's pot. Perhaps the woman could understand. He made the hand signs for eating, but her eyes blazed and her voice snapped at him like a bullwhip, calling him a pagan devil. He could take her scalp, she said; she couldn't stop him. But he would have her body only after she was dead.

Joseph understood most of this. He turned away, feeling the blood beat in his veins. These white eyes . . . Let them starve, then. He retired to the other side of the fire, where a canvas was hung in the brush to break the wind. Slowly he drank the broth which he had set aside for the prisoners, and stared over the flame. His eyes were glazed by the exhaustion of endless flight. He didn't want that white woman. He wouldn't take her as a gift. Her pale-blue jelly eyes were so light they must be nearly blind. In her narrow wolf's jaw there wasn't room for a decent set of human teeth, and her face had the unhealthy paleness of flour paste. He imagined her body, sour and dead white all over. One only had to look at that poor creature, or at her brother with his scraggly goat's beard, to know they had sprung from impure stock, some mongrel breed from God knew where. Indians were clearly the original people. One need only look at their hair, always black; at their dark eyes and their burnished skins. The whites were blotched as the hybrid appaloosa. Why did they come so far into this land of mountains and forest to imprison themselves in smoky cabins? Why did they come with their Sabbath souls to preach of heaven and hell and Christian brotherhood, and then to drive the Indians from their homes? "I am weary of their faces," he thought. "Behind them all, I see savages. This old dog of mine has a better soul than theirs. He is honest and loyal. He limps, but he never complains." Feeling his master's hand, the dog beat his tail on the ground and gaped. From his mouth lolled a long red tongue. "There's nothing in the world that loves like a dog. I wonder why any animal should love a man so much." If he were the omnipotent God of which those white men sang, he would find some other place for their whole tribe—perhaps that hot hell the black robes seemed to love. He would fill the gap they left on earth with dogs.

Round and large the moon rode overhead, casting down sly shadows which seemed to slink and hide among the trees. It was late. Before rolling up in his blanket, Joseph checked his carbine, working its lever to be sure. From across the glow of the fire, the white woman drew a quick breath as he did so.

Mist came before dawn and with it arrived a thin chill rain. Presently the captive girl began to moan. Joseph awoke and listened, telling himself her minor suffering gave him pleasure. It did not, and presently he sent Singing Beads to build up the sputtering fire. He told her to put a bit of canvas over the girl's shoulders against the damp, and this she did. By now the dawn breeze blew through the trees with a sad murmurous voice, and the autumn rain crept with frosty fingers inside his blanket. He walked down to the creek and found it crusted razor-thin with ice. Only in the center did the current still move sluggishly.

At first light, he took the captives bowls of hot broth. No hand signals now, no talking. They received the bowls in silence, and the girl did not look at him. Before setting out on the day's trek, Joseph conferred with Poker Joe. They agreed it was better to release the tourists before the hotheaded young braves had their way, so they took them to the forest edge. "You will not be followed," Joseph said. "Now go. We make no war on women." Not understanding, they looked as though they expected to be scalped. "Here," he said, holding out a claw from the grizzly shot in Montana. "You take it. Come. Take it." Ida Carpenter approached and extended her hand as though the gift were a hot coal. "Take it, daughter. It can't bite." So she took the present with an uncertain smile and then returned to the security of her companions. "She is Spring Song's age," he thought, "yet so much younger. I could not hurt her." But judging by the way the tourists flung themselves into the forest, they must have expected arrows to whistle in pursuit.

Not all the tourists in the Yellowstone were as fortunate. At Mammoth Hot Springs on the last day of August, a photographer was waiting beside his tripod for the geyser display when he was surprised by Toohoolhoolzote's braves. He died in screaming flight. They left his body to boil in one of the handy mud pots there. A German piano teacher, Richard Dietrich, was cornered in the Mammoth Springs Hotel by the same wild bunch. They killed him, experimented with a few discordant notes on his piano, and broke it up before leaving. Late in the day they came upon a final group of tourists, the Helena party. Ben Stone, the Negro cook for the expedition, was preparing supper when the Indians appeared. He mistook them at first for a herd of elk. When guns began going off, Ben somersaulted down into an icy river and saved his scalp. It was a part of his anatomy for which he had great concern, since the local Indians were said to regard a black man's hair as good medicine for sore ears. Most of the party were off hunting at the time. Only Charlie Kench, caught sleeping at the camp, was killed in cold blood, one more tally on the vengeance scroll for the Nez Percé murdered at the Big Hole. Joseph opposed these roving bands, but they were Toohoolhoolzote's braves, stirred by his Messianic ravings. Their ears were not entirely stopped to Joseph's words, for they took no scalps, nor did they injure women or children while passing through the Yellowstone.

All this while, Bannock scouts had kept close behind, their ranks thinned by desertion as the opportunities to steal horses diminished. It was easier to steal from the Army, which, according to Nez Percé outriders, had delayed near Henry Lake. Howard was waiting for supplies of food and winter clothes to come up from Virginia City.

As August gave way to September's smoky sunshine,

the Nez Percé moved slowly from Yellowstone Lake up Pelican Creek and over the Mist Creek Pass. Then they struggled north again, following Mist Creek through a land choked with granite boulders and fallen pine. This was even harder on the stock than the Bitterroot Mountains had been, and many horses and mules were left dead or hopelessly crippled.

Heading east again through more open country, they made for the old Bannock Trail. According to Poker Joe, this led toward the open plains beyond the Clark's Fork divide. But first the gorge narrowed. For uncounted centuries, the river had sawn into the rock, cutting more sharply than the blow of a tomahawk. The defile was scarcely a hundred yards wide, and yellow-gray walls rose sheer and twice as high on either side. On the second day in the chasm, when their commitment there was absolute, a tracker, He Who Knows the Marks, brought word to the chiefs that the way was blocked. Colonel Sturgis, having received the call over the singing wire, waited outside the Clark's Fork exit with six companies of the Seventh Cavalry. He was spoiling to avenge the Custer massacre at the Little Big Horn the year before.

Even should they climb out of the canyon, and there were places where this could be done, beyond its rim rose impossible mountains. A few braves might straggle through, but they would leave behind a broken people. They would take with them only the prospect of being hunted down by troopers in the winter, which had already touched the mountain peaks with snow.

There was wild and desperate talk. Toohoolhoolzote was for flinging himself upon Sturgis in a last battle. Another suggestion was to send out raiding parties to fire the woods around the troopers—but the forest might not burn after the recent rains. Besides, it was a good friend and a refuge. "There may be another way," said Joseph. "I have talked with He Who Knows the Marks. Now hear me." With a stick he marked out a plan in the dirt.

"Not even a white man would be fooled by such a trick," chided Looking Glass. Since the Camas Meadows, he had the younger braves behind him. They wanted a fight to the finish.

"It will work," Ollokot insisted.

"If it does not work, then you will have your last battle," Joseph added.

So it was decided.

The plan was simple enough. With two narrow exits from the Absaroka Mountains—one at Clark's Fork, the other at the north fork of the Stinking Water River—Sturgis must be made to expect them at the wrong one. The trick lay only in the execution of this deception.

At the first easy path, they climbed to the canyon's rim, then climbed again from there to the top of Dead Indian Hill. From here Joseph could see the open prairies six miles away, and, farther to the east by some sixty miles, the smoking peaks of the Big Horn Mountains. At this point, Joseph calculated, they were within an hour's ride of Sturgis and his troopers, who were reported to be encamped on the northern slope of Heart Mountain watching Clark's Fork. Aware that from the forest the Bannocks must also be watching, the Nez Percé set out from Dead Indian Hill in a direct line toward the course of the Stinking Water. For two miles they kept on, until, helped by the lowering mist and the dense woods, they milled their horses while a few braves rode on noisily. The others, led by Joseph, filtered back under heavy cover to a deep drainage basin known as Dead Indian Gulch. This cut in the cliffs fell one thousand feet in the space of a mile. Under the sheltering pines, their horses' hoofs were muffled by the deep floor of needles. They progressed slowly. The ground fell away. Farther down, flash floods had cut savagely. There was no horizon. Stony walls echoed back every sound, and the shadows were as profound as the last twilight. Six hundred Indians and over a thousand laden mules and ponies slid and staggered to the rocky floor of the canyon. The walls rose twelve hundred feet on either side. There was no escape, so they forced the ponies and forced themselves down the narrow gorge, which was as dark as a railway tunnel.

This is either the beginning of something or the end, thought Joseph. With most of the braves still riding decoy, they stood no chance in the widening "V" of Clark's Fork should Sturgis still be there. Perhaps the Bannock scouts had all defected. Then their ruse would have gone unnoticed. Perhaps they had been observed too closely. Then Sturgis, the old Indian hater whose son had died at the Little Big Horn, would be waiting to destroy them.

Ollokot and Joseph rode ahead the last mile, followed by Joseph's big, grave, sleepy-eyed dog. The plain widened before them. It was the old grazing ground of the buffalo. Mile after mile rolled into the haze, and there was not a living creature in sight.

So the Nez Percé passed out of the mountains of the Yellowstone into the plains, where the north wind came no longer in fitful gusts but unrelentingly, with nothing to stop it. Turning north, still following the Yellowstone River, they headed for the narrow passage of Canyon Creek. Scouts were on the lookout for Sturgis and for buffalo. They found instead the Canyon Creek stage station, arriving there at the same time as the westbound stage, an ancient two-seater affair called a jerky. Yellow paint scabbed from its sides. The passenger, a full-bosomed vaudeville performer named Fanny Clark, escaped into the brush with petticoats flying. The driver was right behind her. Only the mail did not get away. Fearing messages to Howard, the Indians scattered it like confetti on the prairie wind. Then fourteen braves boarded the creaking stage and set out hooting and ki-yipping after the Nez Percé column. The stage horses were driven into a panting lather. Finally, all was abandoned when a wheel spun off and the jerky broke up. It was a small but pleasing victory over the white world of wheels and wires and iron rails.

For some time there was no sign of the troopers. The only trace of buffalo were great lumps of dry dung telling of the uncounted millions that had roamed these plains short years before. So rapid was their disappearance that it was easy to believe the story of evil Red Old Man, who had herded the buffalo up into the mountains and hidden them from the people. In the story, they were saved from starvation by White Old Man, who found them and brought them back. But now the medicine men who prayed to the sun and the moon to help find the lost herds prayed in vain. Joseph had gone only rarely to the buffalo hunt, but he knew better than the legends. He had seen the long caravans of wagons and the white hunters who could kill a whole buffalo herd in a day. It took only seven minutes to slash off a skin, an afternoon to fill a wagon with blood-dripping hides. He had seen these white hunters take a tongue or two for supper and leave the rest to turn into black heaps of decay sizzling with flies. That was where the buffalo had gone, and with them had dwindled the Indians of the plains, who had killed sparingly and used what they had killed: flesh for food; hides for clothes; tipis, and armor; bones for needles and weapons; sinew for thread; entrails for carrying sacks; hoofs for glue. Even the slow-burning buffalo chips had warmed their winter lodges. But now all but the chips and the bleaching bones were gone.

Along the banks of the Yellowstone, they were joined by Ollokot and the braves he had used to decoy the Army. They'd be followed soon. In fact, upon the southern horizon moving specks already announced the approach of the Seventh Cavalry. From then on, it was a race to the Judith Gap, with the cavalry gaining all the way and the braves trying to slow them down long enough for the women and children to crowd into the canyon's narrow entrance. Sturgis had his chance to cut them off, but he had heard of the Nez Percé marksmanship, and ghosts of the Little Big Horn still danced in his head. His troops advanced slowly and on foot. Captain Frederick Benteen, a veteran of the Little Big Horn, rode in hard at the last, turning the Indians' flank, but by then warriors had scaled the bluffs on either side of the canyon mouth and held its approaches in a cross fire. Three soldiers were killed and eleven wounded trying to undo Sturgis's caution. The Nez Percé had two braves killed and lost uncounted horses in the scrambling dash into Judith Gap.

The cavalry was stopped dead, but a few braves could not close the gap indefinitely. They held out that night and well into the following day. All this time Joseph drove his people north toward the Missouri. Some hoped for Crow warriors to join them, but the prairie, gone red as sunset for as far as the eye could see, was empty. There the autumn wind played like the sighing of ghosts.

The horses were dropping regularly now. Even the war ponies were carrying baggage. Travois had for the most part been abandoned. Many of the people walked. A few squaws were reduced to carrying their possessions with burden straps about their foreheads. Singing Beads and Spring Song walked together and took turns carrying the baby on her cradle board. Dusk fell, and with the passing of the light the cold intensified. Still they trekked on. Joseph rode along the column until he came to his family. There he dismounted and urged Singing Beads to ride. She refused. The moonlight fell full upon her, searching out her drawn and haggard features. When she raised her eyes to his, they were neither joyful nor sad, simply dull. He forced her to ride then, walking himself beside Spring Song. She was like her father, always with a last reserve of energy. His old dog followed them. The cold had stiffened him. He moved painfully, but he still had a strong bark. Like the rest, he was not ready to give up. But the prairie seemed endless. Joseph peered ahead into the emptiness and felt a vast weariness behind his eyes. The troopers must feel it, too—the cold and the lengthening miles.

The troopers, in their summer blues, were feeling it all right, but, like the wolf pack running down a stag, they had hunters to spare and came on in panting relays. Next day it was fifty fresh Bannocks—painted red and yellow, their horses' tails dyed green and decked with sleigh bells—who led the pursuit, having been promised as many of Joseph's horses as they could run off. That day the first Crows of the Absaroka tribe arrived. They hand-signaled for a conference. Looking Glass had long regarded them as allies against the Army, and he rode out to confer, together with Joseph and Spring Song. A volley of arrows greeted them before Ollokot could ride up with his braves to put them to rout.

No damage was done except to Spring Song, who received an arrow through her left arm. She looked more surprised than hurt.

"Now I know what it is like," she said. Joseph reached for a knife. "What are you going to do, Father?"

"It has to come out," he told her. The knife was made of sheet metal, and dull. In the end, he had to snap the arrow's shaft and drew it out. Spring Song took a quick breath as he did so, and her eyes squinted shut. She did not cry out or move her arm away, and the pain she felt shot through his own heart. He held her arm carefully. "It bleeds," he said. "Enough, but not too much. Come. We still have some of Strike Standing's medicine."

"You may need it if there is another battle," she said.

"We will use it now," he told her with finality and with husky pride. She had the heart of a warrior, that daughter of his.

All that day the Crow and Bannocks harassed the flanks of the Nez Percé column. They had cut out several hundred horses before Ollokot took his warriors and punished them. Beaten, they fell back, waiting for the troopers. One Crow brave was taken captive. The Boy That Grabs, they called him, and some wanted his scalp. But Joseph put him on a lame horse, saw him quirted over the head a few times, and told him to tell his people they were old women who ought to mind their lodges until the white men took them away. There was savage pleasure in this, and yet the hope of a refuge among the Crows had been dashed. Joseph had never really held this hope, nor had Poker Joe, but some of the old and weary had counted on an end of their troubles here. They began to lose heart. A few dropped out of the column, but Joseph encouraged the others. The mountains were behind them now. They had only to cross the Missouri River and then the way lay open before them. Three days of hard travel, perhaps four, and they would cross that invisible line beyond which Howard, Sturgis, and any troopers who followed them could not pass.

X
Cow Island

Frost glittered on the prairie like slivers of glass. Ahead rose black autumn clouds, full of rain or snow. A cold wind cut across Joseph's face, tugging his hair, caressing the dark-brown scar on his forehead that felt tight and dead. It would turn from brown to blue, and one day, if he lived long enough, all that would remain would be a silvery trace. He worried more about Spring Song's arm.

"It's nothing," she told him. "Look." She worked all her fingers. "I'd take an arrow in my other wrist for some buffalo meat."

"I'll send the hunters out soon," he promised. For days now he had felt hunger inside him, and each night he had known he must sleep with it again—not only with the hunger, but with a weariness of arms and legs that made his joints feel lubricated with hot sand. How the horses kept going, he did not know. Most of the survivors were so thin their bones looked about to work out through their hides, yet each morning they set out like so many clumsy statues in motion. And if the Crows or Bannocks came whooping down with tomahawks brandished, they would not roll their eyes or shake their heads or hurry any faster. If he were the Great Spirit, he would bring back the horses along with the dogs to a better world. They were calm and uncomplaining. They did not quarrel or lie awake in the dark plotting against their fellows.

They never worried over the future, regretted the past, or counted their sins. They did not kneel to one another; they dug no gold, built no fences, killed no living thing.

Beyond Big Spring Creek, a few horses were taken from the Crows. A ranch herd was also appropriated, and with the major burdens shifted over to these fresh animals, the Nez Percé were able to press stubbornly on to the south bank of the Missouri River. The Seloselo Wejanwais, as the Indians called the Missouri, was the last natural barrier before Canada. They reached it on the twenty-third day of September. Looking Glass favored a rest and a buffalo hunt. Joseph was for crossing first. "We will talk of stopping on the other side," he insisted. "Let us put the water between us and Howard." So it was decided, and the Nez Percé headed down the last bleak, eroded miles through the badlands south of the river to where it was fordable near Cow Island.

In late summer, the water was so shallow here that the steamer could go no farther, so Cow Island served as a cargo point for Fort Benton. There was no permanent structure on the island, only a tent for the guardians of the government stores—two sergeants, one corporal, nine privates, and four civilians.

While Joseph reconnoitered the bank for the best place to cross, Ollokot and some braves splashed ahead to the island. There they offered to buy food. The sergeants conferred. It seemed an opportunity for easy money, but they might be court-martialed if they took advantage of it. At first they refused, but in the end, out of mixed sympathy and fear, they gave Ollokot a side of bacon and a sack of hardtack. It didn't go far among starving people. A few gorged and became ill on raw bacon, but most of them got nothing. When darkness fell, Toohoolhoolzote stirred up his braves, who attacked the island through the willows. The soldiers fired back and then fled. The braves got into the whiskey first. They were drunk and setting fires before they tackled the food, most of which was scattered or burned. All that they salvaged in quantity were two hundred bags of sugar, and in the process much travel time was wasted and the alarm went out.

The Nez Percé, quarreling over the distribution of sugar, did not move next morning until long after the sun came up bleeding red and orange as through an open wound. It seemed a bad omen to Joseph, who usually put little store by omens. That was for old women and exhorters. But he was more than ever anxious for the trail. Not until midmorning were the last families moving up Cow Creek Canyon. Sulphur-gray wolves followed after. It was crippled horses they wanted.

Toward midday the Indians began overtaking a bull train of some fifteen wagons coupled in twos and threes and drawn by oxen. The braves, with Poker Joe, tried to purchase ammunition. They were refused, but the mood was genial enough. Poker Joe asked where good grass for grazing might be found, and a spontaneous camp was being set up near the wagons before Joseph could arrive and prevent it. Hunters went out and had no luck. The distant campfire of the bullwhackers was watched narrowly by the hungry braves that night. They imagined the wagons full of beef and bullets, and, before the first trace of dawn, Toohoolhoolzote was egging on his braves once more. The bullwhackers were ready for them. The fight enlarged. Looking Glass approved it, and so they dueled all that morning in open ground. Noon came and Joseph could not stop it. Blood was up on both sides, and not until the whites retreated and their wagons were taken did the braves break off. Flour was scattered on the wind, a few bullets were found, and all the rest was burned. A pair of oxen were slaughtered for food. Then, with evening already in the sky, Joseph set them on the trail once more. Precious hours had again been wasted.

More would be. Looking Glass, whose star had been ascendant among the younger warriors ever since the Camas Meadow fight, insisted on holding a council. "One-Armed Howard is far behind," he said. There was weariness in his tone and in the pink rims of his eyes. "We must have time to eat and rest. Do we wish to come to Sitting Bull without horses? Without pride? All bones and empty bellies? No, I say. Let the hunters go out."

Poker Joe, who had led them since the Big Hole, wanted to press on, even though he was not a Nez Percé. "In two days . . . maybe three . . . we will be in the Land of the Old Lady. There you may hunt without fear."

Joseph backed him up. "We have lost a day's lead by fighting over flour. One-Armed Howard is behind us."

"Far behind us," interjected Looking Glass.

"And the Seventh Cavalry."

"They have been beaten before."

"Grandfather, don't forget the Big Hole. Don't forget the click-clack and the singing wire. We have taken dispatches from the Crow messengers to Fort Benton calling out the foot soldiers."

"Let them walk in our dust."

"They have horses, fresher than ours, grandfather. And from down the Tongue River where the sun rises, fresh troopers are riding. Bear-Coat Miles leads them. I have heard it."

"Joseph has heard it," repeated Looking Glass. "Joseph says he has heard it. Who is this Bear Coat? Must we fear the bear's coat now and not his claws? Joseph, I do not jest with you. My people are weary. Your people are hungry. Our ponies are raw. Their legs are thin, and they shake like sticks in the cold wind. We must hunt or starve. If we press on without food, we will leave half our herd for the wolves and the Bannocks, and many scalps. Joseph, hunger crawls through my belly like a long-legged worm. You are younger than I am, cousin, but are you not hungry, too? Is your wife not hungry? Ask her. Ask Toohoolhoolzote about his people. Let White Bird speak."

Toohoolhoolzote sat down on a hummock of earth. He supported himself with an outstretched hand. He was too old to be a warrior. He had reached the age when a chief should puff his pipe and give advice. If he had to run any more, his body would fail. "Let us travel more slowly, but let us send out hunters. The hunters will be as scouts to warn us of the soldiers' coming. What does it matter if it takes three days or four?"

Next White Bird, who had all along yearned for Canada, had his say. The events of these last days had chiseled a look of bewilderment upon his face. His voice was soft and husky, and his exhaustion weighed on every slow and labored word. "We must go to the Land of the Old Lady," he said. "I have always believed that. But I am old, and my people are starving. Let us go now, but let us go slowly. I agree with my brother, Toohoolhoolzote." White Bird had spoken. Before he rose, he closed his eyes as if the firelight hurt them. In that moment, he looked disturbingly like a corpse.

Last of all, Poker Joe rose to speak again. The crease between his brows had deepened. The corners of his mouth were turned down. "Very well," he said. "I have tried to save your people. I have done my best to lead you to Canada before the soldiers finish us all. Now Looking Glass returns to take command. Let him. But I think we will all be caught and killed."

In this way, Looking Glass once more became chief over all, and though the Nez Percé moved camp that day, they did not move far and they settled down long before the early dusk. Hunters went out. The snow on the distant mountains sparkled like hammered silver. All went well. Mule deer were hunted down to the river and shot as they swam. Even a buffalo was taken. The omens were good, and with the return of the hunters, sentinels were posted. That was one mistake even Looking Glass would not make again. As the supper fires began to glow, a shot rang out. Joseph stood up, ready to fight. But it was only the taking of one last mule deer.

They ate well that night, all of them. There was fat left over for the old dog, whose legs had taken to trembling like reeds in the cold. They slept well, too. Even Joseph, snug beneath a spread canvas, was untroubled by dreams.

XI

The Camp at Bear Paw

Thirty miles from the Canadian border the Little Rockies and the Bear Paw Mountains draw close to one another. It was toward the pass between the two ranges that the Nez Percé headed. Isolated buffalo were seen during the day, and hunters pursued them. A Cheyenne scout named Brave Wolf talked to the hunters and told them he had seen soldiers. The hunters replied that they would fight to the death before any soldiers would take them. This was all done in sign language. As they neared the Place of the Manure Fires, a favorite camping spot because of the buffalo chips available there, a lone soldier was spotted. Ollokot gave halfhearted chase, but the soldier, on a fresh horse, got away. Clearly they were still being observed, but what did that matter? They had been spied upon every day for the last three months.

In mid-afternoon they camped at the Place of the Manure Fires. Flanked by the first bluffs of the Bear Paw range, the whole scene was flat and without depth, like a scene painted on a buffalo hide. Joseph did not like it. He did not like this country at all. He felt stripped and plundered by its bleak emptiness and the searching Arctic wind which played through the eroded ravines. But there was water and protection in the depressions carved by wind and rain. Joseph's people camped in the most southerly part. North of them were Looking Glass, White Bird, and Toohoolhoolzote. Poker Joe camped with Joseph. Around each camp, sentinels dug rifle pits. If the white-eyes came, they would not be taken by surprise a second time.

Again the hunters went out under swollen blue-gray clouds that rolled from the northwest. They brought back deer and buffalo, and they told the children: "Go cry to the thunders." And the children gathered outside and sang: "O Great Spirits, we thank you. Here we are, giving thanks."

The council met that night in a good mood. Looking Glass said they should stay another day, taking meat to smoke for the winter ahead. But the others wished to press on. Sioux scouts had been seen. Some of the hunters had met a party of Assiniboines—walk-around Sioux, as the Nez Percé called them—who had said soldiers were near and might attack them at any time.

"We are ready for them," said Looking Glass. "One more battle will do us good." Few shared his fighting spirit now. It was too cold. Winter was near, and when the exhorter spoke, he told of snow on its way. None wanted to be caught in a blizzard. Joseph waited for White Bird to speak, and then he noticed all eyes were upon him. This time he spoke with confidence as one who has overcome a long illness. "One more day. One more hard day on the trail tomorrow, and then all will be well." Except for Looking Glass, they were all behind him, but Looking Glass blew out his cheeks like the gas-inflated belly of a dead buffalo.

"Look at the grandfather," said one of the braves. "He is full of raw meat and gas. When the soldiers come,

THE CAMP AT BEAR PAW 189

he will blow them away." This ended the last council. At first light they would set out. They would not stop again until they had passed into the safety of Queen Victoria's land.

Feeling more relief than he could remember, Joseph returned to the wind-cut depression where his family had set up their temporary canvas lodge. Sentinels were out. All seemed well. Regret for their homeland would never leave them, but at least tomorrow there would be an end to fear.

He told the good news to his women. "Before the Sunbearer leaves us again, we will be safe."

"No more trekking?" asked Singing Beads.

"No more."

"I can work on my willow baskets?"

"I will cut the willow for you," he promised. "I will hunt. You will teach Spring Song to cure the skins."

"It will be like home."

"No one knows," he said, "but it will be better than running from Howard."

Suddenly with a shout he snatched up the baby and swung her joyfully around. "Wife," he shouted, "I am hungry." He knew full well there was plenty: venison pressed out between flat boards; buffalo tongue spitted over the fire and dripping juice. As each drop landed, the flames shot high. The meat browned and crinkled. "Smell it," he said. "How beautiful."

They ate until the tears ran from their eyes—until nothing was left. Let tomorrow take care of itself. Then, in the warm glow of the buffalo-chip fire, they lay down together to sleep. The baby fed last at Singing Beads's breast. Through it all, she had kept her milk, and the baby closed her eyes into thin drugged crescents. A contented bubble formed on her lips and would not burst. The old dog was sated, too. He continued to pant for some time, and one hind leg trembled. Finally his eyes closed, his breathing relaxed, and he slept. An occasional shudder passed through him. Joseph lay beside Singing Beads. Her hair had blown across her smiling mouth, and her slow breathing reminded him of spring meadows in the Wallowa.

Joseph tried to sleep, but blood thumped in his temples. His skin was hot and dry. His mind pored over the past and future, and his legs twitched, trying to walk like the dreaming dog's. It was hopeless. He extended his hand to cover Singing Beads's body, which lay under his fingers like the fragile form of a frightened animal. His touch did not disturb her, and she did not wake when he rose. He left the makeshift tipi. The flap fell behind him.

The wind whistled and drummed in the dark like a herd of wild horses, and Joseph was oppressed by the sudden cheerless emptiness of the world. It was that cold night hour when human hearts seem to slow and life is reluctant to proceed. He leaned against the gnarled trunk of a dead tree. It rested him and gave him comfort. He felt its branches about him, and he thought of his father. The wind made the tree whisper, and he yearned to converse with it. In the old days, trees were said to have spoken, but not in his lifetime. A bobcat passed low to the ground, glinted her eyes, and was gone on the wind.

Guards were out. He could trust them, so what was he doing here? A sound like the crunching of a twig underfoot distracted him. He felt for the knife at his belt, breathed deep. Then a dark shadow moved against the lesser darkness of the night. It came toward him, taking form.

"Brother," he exclaimed, "what brings you out in the cold?"

"And what of you, grandfather?"

Neither smiled, but both seemed on the verge of doing so.

"I don't like the sky tonight," said Joseph.

"You are right. Everything is too quiet."

"Except the wind. It brings a he-cold."

"If I could hear an owl or a fox . . ."

There came a whistling overhead like sudden wind in pine tops.

"Geese," said Joseph. "Flying south."

Ollokot looked upward and nodded. "Grandfather, it is a storm wind that brings them. Feel the cold."

"It is the month of the little Snow Moon. Even in the Wallowa, the snow will come."

"Smell it on the wind. The clouds move fast. Hear them sing."

The wind was traveling high and hard.

Joseph said: "The summer was short. Never can I remember such a short summer."

"Yes, but the sun will return. Even in the Land of the Old Lady."

"Brother, for you the sun shines anywhere," Joseph said. As long as he could depend on Ollokot, the sun would not entirely set. He could even look forward to winter in Canada—to the silence, and the deep drifting snow, and the heavy green of the pines. In every land it was the same snow, and in every land the same icy stars looked down. Yet for Joseph there was a difference. Tonight the stars whispered to him of the Wallowa. His homesickness formed its own images, replacing the dark barren landscapes.

"Grandfather, you should sleep," Ollokot said. "Tomorrow you lead us again."

"Are you trying to get rid of me, brother?"

"Sometimes I have thought the whites would get rid of us both."

"As long as we're both alive, they will never defeat us," said Joseph. Ollokot could never be defeated. Not even the white man could defeat a happy Indian, and in Ollokot's eyes was that perpetual flash of gaiety which, for Joseph, remained a warranty of survival.

"Grandfather, I believe you."

They gripped each other's hands, hard. On both their faces glowed an inextinguishable determination of purpose.

"The night grows colder. Come with me," Joseph said.

"Where are we going?"

"I'm not sure. I'm lost, too."

THE CAMP AT BEAR PAW 193

They walked once round the small camp of their people. On what seemed the rim of the last wilderness, all seemed well.

Returning to his makeshift lodge, Joseph slipped inside, lay down, and was quickly asleep. He slept hard and mindlessly to awake groggily when the dog put his nose to his master's ear, uttering thin whining sounds as if he had a message that was important and secret. "I don't want to wake you, Father," he seemed to say. "Father, you said when the dawn came." The voice no longer belonged to the dog. It was Spring Song, her hand on Joseph's shoulder. He rolled up on his elbow. The dog had a sneezing attack, then gazed at the waking man with rapt adoration. He gave a great stretch, and a mouth-gaping yawn. Joseph pressed his fingers against his eyes, drawing his hands down. A pale yellow trace along the black horizon told him the Sunbearer was approaching. He could hardly believe it. Never before had he fallen back on his daughter's prompting, and on so important a morning. He managed a smile for the concerned look in her eyes, and arose without disturbing his wife or the baby.

Together they went outside. The air made him gasp. Surely it would snow before nightfall. Frost fell on his face like tiny pinpricks, and the embers of many fires, some stirred into new life by the squaws, contested with the dawn. Whiskey-jacks pecked at scraps and flew down to steal food from the fires.

They left the depression where the camp was set up and walked toward the herd of horses. Some braves joined them. Spring Song led the way with long, springing strides. She moved like a reed in the breeze.

"How will this Land of the Old Queen be?" she asked.

"Cold," said Joseph. "Cold . . . We will see. There will be more game there, I think."

"Will Ta-Tanpkah-ye-tan-kah help us?" She referred to Sitting Bull by his Indian name.

"He was once our enemy," Joseph replied. "Now we both flee the white man. He will help, I think."

"Look. There is a deer feeding with the horses."

One of the braves raised his carbine, but Joseph made him lower the muzzle. "There is no time," he said. But what he could not bear was the thunder of the shot in that icy stillness, the thought of the pain and the blood. The deer switched its tail, raised its head, and sprang away. By now the sun lay along the horizon, giving no more warmth than the polar star. Shreds of coppery clouds veiled it. A single star, blinking like a chip of ice in the west, winked and went out. The new day had come.

As they approached, the dark mass of the herd separated into phantom horses. Ghostly braves walked among them, cutting out those which could carry loads for a long day from those which could at best keep up. Already many were loaded and the pack train was under way, moving off toward Canada.

Nothing would delay them now. It was not really happiness, but a relief of mind that made Joseph sing without even knowing it.

THE CAMP AT BEAR PAW 195

"What song is that, Father?" Spring Song asked him.

"Was I singing? . . . I think it is one of your grandfather's songs, about riding like the west wind . . . There are our horses." The big appaloosa on which he had raced Ollokot in better days stood before the others. The trail had not broken him down. His feet were spread, his neck arched, and his eyes rolled sideways in watchful alarm. His ears were back. He still had spirit. He could be dangerous. Spring Song walked straight up to him and put her hand on his nose.

"Watch out for his teeth."

Spring Song stroked the long muzzle. The ears began to move forward.

Joseph looked over his lesser mounts. He wanted to leave none behind, for even those which arrived crippled in Canada could be food when it was most needed.

They had broken out their horses and were about to lead them back when Spring Song stiffened like a deer listening for danger. Dropping to his knees, Joseph pressed his ear to the ground. Above the whisper of the wind came the sound of hoofs. Buffalo? The noise was like the roll of muffled tom-toms. Hard, round hoofbeats of many horses. An icy fist seemed to contract around Joseph's heart. At first he saw only women running back from skinning the last of the buffalo. Behind and among them rode a few braves, all bound for the camp. Then on the wind he heard the high brassy sound of a bugle.

At full gallop the cavalry poured in, like the sea, yelling and bugling. They swept toward the herd, a jagged wave of foaming horses' heads and brandished sabers.

Joseph had his carbine up and was firing. He pulled the trigger with a fierce grunt as though striking each time with a tomahawk. The troopers drove into them. Joseph's horse sprang away as if lightning had exploded in his hoofs. Spring Song reached out for him. For an instant her face and arms gleamed in the dust, her eyes wide with panic. Then she was gone beneath the stampede. Hoofs flew at Joseph's face. Struck down, he groveled on all fours, the carbine lost. The appaloosa appeared again beside him, its head rearing, eyes glaring, legs trampling the air. The old dog, screaming through yellow teeth, dragged himself out of range.

As suddenly as they had come, the troopers were gone. Joseph struggled to his feet. His head was splitting and he moved his hand around his ear, then to the back of his neck. It was sticky, but there was no hole—no excuse for giving up, no easy escape into death. He stood up, shivering. About him were strewn horses and a few men, Indians and troopers together, but most of them were gone with the dying thunder of hoofs. He saw it all too clearly. In that moment of horror his mind stood apart, calm, unquestioning, seeing it all from a distance. The attack had already reached the main camp in an unbroken wave until they were met there by a rippling volley. Protected by the eroded landscape, the Nez Percé had been ready. Horses reared, toppled, ran back riderless. The first charge was broken, but with it had gone over half of the Nez Percé herd.

Not far away Joseph saw his appaloosa. It was standing on three legs, and beside it lay Spring Song. He ran to her, but before he could help her she rose unsteadily to her feet. A few others, braves and horses, were picking themselves up from what had seemed a field of the dead. Joseph gathered the braves together and ordered them to overtake and protect the supply column that was already on the trail to Canada. Then he turned to Spring Song. She had his own proud lean looks, the same high-bridged nose and long limbs. She was not really beautiful. She was trail-worn and pinched by the cold. Yet to Joseph she had never seemed more lovely, his fierce son and gentle daughter all in one.

"You must go with them," he told her.

Her eyes flashed back at him like those of an animal at bay. She would not leave him.

"If you die," he said slowly, "it will be for your father like being blinded." He knew if she went back to the embattled camp, if she were captured and confined by the whites, she would die as wild things do in cages. He found her an ugly, hammer-headed horse, still strong and trail-worthy with a sinewy play of muscle in legs and chest. No fear but that it could carry her safe to the border.

"I want you to tell the Sioux," he said. "Tell Sitting Bull we need help. Hurry." He did not really believe that the Sioux would come. No Indians had come to their aid before. But it would help his daughter to feel that she was doing something for the tribe—and there was always a chance.

They were parting, possibly forever, and each wished to show deep fondness with more than words. But there was no time, and between these two it was unnecessary. Joseph slapped the old horse across its rump, and his tall daughter, her heavy black hair flying, rode off after the braves. She sat upright. She has shoulders like a warrior, he thought, as she rode away into the morning.

His heart yearned to ride with her, but even if Singing Beads and the baby had been safe in Victoria's land, he could not have gone. Not while his people needed him. Joseph searched about for his gun. The muzzle was clogged with dirt, but otherwise it was sound. Then he went after his horse. It would give him one last ride into camp. After that he would need the appaloosa no more. On the way he found the dog. It lay on its side, panting heavily. He moved the dog's hind legs slowly. They would no longer move by themselves. He knelt down and held the dog's head in his lap. "You're a faithful old friend," he said. The dog tried to lick his face, but the tail could no longer wag. He had no bullets to spare and he would need them. Yet for an old friend he would use one. Holding the dog's eyes with his own, he fired the carbine with one hand. "No more hurt," he said, almost wishing he could do the same for himself. Then he rose and mounted his pony. The cavalry had pulled back, those that survived the first charge, and he drew only a few distant shots. His face bore an expression of fixed calm as though his soul no longer dwelt behind it. It was more the face of a carved totem, tranquil, yet terrible as a shaman's mask, as he rode into the Nez Percé camp.

XII
Death at Bear Paw

The Nez Percé had been at their campfires when the attack began. Tom Hill, a mixed-blood, saw the stampeded herd and gave the warning. Looking Glass rode through camp, calming the people. "Plenty time, plenty time." He had urged the children to eat their fill. He would have this last good fight from the ravines and hastily scooped rifle pits. Let the soldiers come.

Three companies of old Colonel Samuel Sturgis's Seventh Cavalry struck first at the south corner of the camp. Their horses rode into a murderous fire. One hundred and fifteen troopers made up that first attack. Fifty-three were cut down. Behind them stormed in the mounted Fifth Infantry. They, too, were driven back. A Hotchkiss gun was brought up. Before a round was fired, the Nez Percé picked off its crew, and the gun was abandoned in retreat. But Joseph knew the battle had just begun. It was not Howard but Bear-Coat Miles who led the fresh troops, and he had heard how Colonel Miles never defended when he could attack. Howard considered the cost in lives each movement would make, and weighed the price. Miles put victory above all else. And so troopers returned. They were in for a death struggle, and they began to dig in. Some advanced cautiously, but they advanced, lumbering like brown bears in their winter greatcoats. Of the officers guiding this assault on the Nez Percé camp, only Lieutenant Eckerson survived. The Fifth Infantry followed them up with long-range rifles. Sniping from a distance, they began to take a toll of the warriors. Poker Joe was one of the first to fall, killed by a Nez Percé sniper who mistook him for a soldier. Toohoolhoolzote of the Dreamer's faith regarded his body as impervious to white man's attack, and he refused to crouch. A storm of shot cut him down and he lay in silence, his clouding eyes full of surprise.

By midday, the snow began falling in small icy flakes that drove like blown sand across the waste. It whirled up into the faces of the Indians. Heavy trade blankets felt thin as paper over their shoulders, and under the thickening clouds the light dimmed. After a while there was no sun. The world was neither light nor dark. It seemed as though the sun were dying.

Counting their casualties, the troopers offered to parley. "Come and take our hair," was Looking Glass's reply, and the soldiers tried. They charged the rifle pits and broke briefly into the southern part of Joseph's camp. He was back from the prairie and in command by then. With Ollokot he drove them out, scarcely noticing the bullet that seared across his leg. He was used to such mementos of fighting, and had ceased to expect a life-taking wound. Even as the bullets twittered by like birds, he strode back and forth, putting heart into his braves, assuring them of the help that was on its way, when he knew no help could come.

When the troopers withdrew, leaving their wounded, he took the fallen soldiers water and blankets. "I don't want your scalps," he reassured the terror-stricken men. "I want your bullets, no more."

Both sides dug in as the snow moved across the prairie, falling on the Bear Paw Mountains and the plains. Quickly it filled in the footprints of men and horses. All was silent except for the moaning of the wind and the wounded. By nightfall, five inches of fresh snow had fallen on the dead.

In full darkness, Joseph and Ollokot inspected the situation.

"It would do us more good to rest," said Ollokot.

"I did not ask you to come, brother."

"I am here."

They went in silence a space, their feet crunching on the hard-trodden snow. In their path lay a corpse, half mantled in white.

"It's laughing. Look!" Ollokot was horrified. "It's laughing at us!"

Pillowed by a drift, the corpse seemed propped on its elbows, eyes and mouth open.

They walked on quickly.

"How is your wound, grandfather?" Ollokot asked.

"The first one hundred wounds hurt the most," Joseph replied. "I have forgotten this one. We must talk of tomorrow . . . There are very few horses left. Not enough for half the people, I think. If we go on foot, and not many can in this snow, Bear-Coat Miles will cut us to pieces. What does Looking Glass say, I wonder?"

"Nothing," Ollokot said. "I saw him. He said nothing.

Tears rolled down his face. Now they say he broods in his tipi in some dream of his ancestors. That one is finished."

"I have heard that. White Bird, too. He dreams of the noose about his neck." Joseph remembered the old chief's exhausted and vacant face, the eyes in which desolation loomed.

"My brother," Joseph said.

"Yes, grandfather."

"I have been thinking."

"Tell me," said Ollokot. "If you asked it, I would give up my grave for you. What do you wish me to do?"

"I was thinking what must happen to those who stay here with me," said Joseph. "One day's ride on a good pony is Sitting Bull. He has two thousand braves."

"You want me to bring them, grandfather? Is that it?"

"You and the warriors who want to go."

"But you will stay?"

"Brother, I must stay with those people who cannot travel."

"Then I stay. We have never gone separate ways. Do not ask me now, brother. Send White Bird, who dreams of being hung. Send that one."

They went to White Bird's camp and found his tipi. The old chief, now in his seventy-fifth winter, lay wrapped in blankets. Only his eyes looked out, and his flabby gourd-like cheeks. Joseph told him what they thought, and White Bird listened. He was afraid to stay and afraid to go. He belched continuously, for it was in his stomach that fear had taken hold. In the end he agreed to go. Two squaws and fourteen braves accompanied him. Most went on foot into the dark, leaving more women, children, and wounded for Joseph to protect.

"Will he bring Sitting Bull, I wonder?" said Ollokot.

"He will try. He is not a bad man," replied Joseph. "Now we must rest and await the sun. I do not want to surrender to this Bear-Coat Miles."

To strengthen the camp, Joseph directed the women to dig trenches and rifle pits. They used their camas hooks and hunting knives as well as trowel bayonets taken from the troopers at the Big Hole. Dug in, they would not give up easily, but Joseph knew that no matter how many soldiers were killed, there would always be more. Even if they were not taken by assault, they could not hold out long with only a few dead horses to eat.

Once the ring of entrenchments was complete, Joseph returned to his tipi. A small fire glowed there, shielded by buffalo robes. He saw the faces of his wife and child; they looked shrunken. The child was growing old too fast. He told himself it was a cruel trick of the firelight. Outside, a camp dog lamented the cold and the bleak loneliness. He raised his nose to the scudding heavens and gave a long sad report on the world as it touched him.

Before the dawn, troopers made a rush and salvaged the abandoned Hotchkiss gun. They were unable to depress the barrel sufficiently and the shots fired at the

Indian camp traveled high overhead. Joseph never heard it. But with the first trace of light, Miles's wagon train came up, bringing a Napoleon cannon, which the troopers set up like a mortar. It belched flame in the dark and sent a shell droning high. It burst at the edge of camp, throwing up a plume of smoke and scattering the snow with dirt. The shots that followed spread alarm, woke the few who slept, but did little harm. Joseph looked up through the smoke vent. The dawn showed gray and cold, promising more snow.

Singing Beads had been awakened by the explosion. She was trying to calm the baby. He put his head on her shoulder and squeezed. "All will be well," he reassured her. "Sitting Bull will come."

"As long as you are alive, I am afraid of nothing," she told him.

"I must go out and be with the braves. It may be the soldiers will attack us again."

Crouching low, Joseph made his way through the wind gullies. Here and there he told hopeful lies to people he met. "All will be well." At the northern edge of the camp, he found Ollokot in the foremost rifle pit. No soldiers were stirring and the cannon had fallen silent.

The brothers embraced.

"What of today, grandfather?" asked Ollokot.

"We wait."

"I have heard Sitting Bull is coming with five thousand braves."

"The people dream," said Joseph. "Perhaps they dream true."

As if in reply to their musing, there was agitation along the trench. Some braves were pointing. Far to the north, black against the snow, shapes moved from the horizon in an endless Indian file. Sitting Bull!

"He has come!" Ollokot shouted, standing for a better look. He had scarcely risen when his body jerked and he sat down backwards as though an invisible hand had driven against his chest. Only then came the echoing report. His lips drew tight over clenched teeth while between his pressed hands oozed a red outpouring. It was a jagged wound laying bare the life within.

"Grandfather," he said, "this is a bad wound." His cheeks blew out from his slow, hard breath. Joseph knelt beside the powerful body into which the dumdum bullet had sunk. "Grandfather, there is a taste in my mouth. It is bitter . . . like the edge of a rusty knife." He clung to Joseph. There was still strength in his hands and arms. "Grandfather, tell me. Does Sitting Bull still come? Do the soldiers run before him?" He was holding himself and his body together by sheer force of will, and the effort showed on his face.

Joseph looked to the horizon. The shapes were nearer now, distinct. "Yes, my brother. Sitting Bull has come with his thousands."

"We are saved. You no longer need me, grandfather."

"Rest yourself. We are saved."

Ollokot's mouth shut in a hard line, refusing to release

the cry that was tearing from within him. He tried to lift his arms to remove the green bottle neck which he had worn so long. The blood poured hotly down his side. His hands failed.

"Keep it. It is yours forever," Joseph told him. "I gave it to you to keep forever."

"In all my days, I have known no one such as you," said Ollokot. "Grandfather, are you still there? . . . Grandfather . . ." His eyes were fixed wide on the wintry sky. They were jet-black, and no midnight in all of Joseph's life would ever be as dark and hopeless as those sightless eyes.

"Ollokot? . . . brother?" He repeated the name again to himself, over and over, denying that his brother's strong young heart could stop, that his songs could be stilled forever. There was a blackness before his own eyes as he whispered his sorrow chant. "I envy you, brother," he said. It seemed all so hopeless now. There would be no clean finality about his own dying. Somehow Joseph knew that. Yet he longed to go with his brother, with that flame that had risen bright and fair and then been snuffed out. But he could not go. The people needed him, and so from deep despair he looked for help. "God, if the Nez Percé have a god, give my body the strength not to desert my soul."

Then he rose to command the warriors in the fight to come, as it would surely come. Nearer now, distinct, no longer black dots, but separate beasts, the buffalo ranged south with the wind at their backs. They had come in their thousands looking for grass, and the Indian file which they had made on the horizon was broken as they grazed in isolated herds upon the bare hillocks blown free of snow. There the wind would not let the snow rest, and it drove icy showers high into the sky, which was empty of birds, empty of all hope for the Nez Percé. As Joseph knelt among his few remaining warriors looking out on this waste, all hope had fled from the world, except the hope of worse to come.

Though gloom wrapped him round, Joseph called a council of the chiefs and war leaders. Few remained. He went personally to bring Looking Glass. For the last day he had sat apart, arms folded, black hat straight on his head, smoking a pipe tomahawk. When Joseph opened the flap of the old warrior's lodge, he found him pitched forward, the top of his head blown off by a stray shot. He had been a force among them, but even before the bullet found him, the plug had been pulled and the determination had gone from him as water runs from a buffalo water bag. The pipe lay splintered in his terrible man-killing hands. Even dying, he had been fighting back.

So no one remained now to question Joseph's leadership at the council. They listened with bowed heads as he told of their dead, and of how Howard was known to be near. Even as he talked, the Napoleon gun lobbed shells into the camp. A squaw and her baby were buried by the explosion. "Looking Glass would tell you, if he were here, that the white man has two faces and speaks with two tongues—that there is no good in a powwow with Bear-Cat Miles. Perhaps Looking Glass is right, but he is dead, and I will speak now with the white man. Does any brave question what I am saying?" There was silence. They were beyond challenges that night, the survivors at the end of the trail.

A white flag was raised. In a moment an answering flag appeared across the waste of snow. Tom Hill, with his mastery of English, went out first to make the arrangements. His singsong returned to Joseph as a wailing part of the icy wind. Then it was up to Joseph. The soldiers awaited him, erect and business-like. He went alone and on foot to face them midway between the hostile camps. "Which one is Bear-Coat Miles?" he asked the interpreter.

"Have you come to surrender?" asked an officer.

"I have come to talk," he replied.

"Surrender first. Then Colonel Miles will hear you."

Joseph turned to go. Clearly they had nothing to say. The soldiers rushed to seize him. Four against one. He made no struggle.

They marched him off to a canvas tent and bound him fast. Joseph lay on the ground, his head supported at an angle by a hummock of earth. He was in the tent alone, and he remained there motionless for some time. Finally two troopers came with water and food. One held a canteen to his lips, but he would not open his mouth. The water ran down his chin. He refused everything.

"Damn-fool Redskin just wants to die," said one.

The other squatted down, looking at Joseph and eating the food that he had refused.

"There's a spirit in some of these Redskins you can't

break. This one gives me the creeps. Hard as a diamond. Look at those eyes." There was in them the stare of an animal turned at bay. "Here, Redskin, have some of this." He held out whiskey. Again Joseph refused. He did not even look up, but suffered them to discuss him as though he were inanimate. "Have it your own way, chief." The soldiers rose. One dropped the empty tin plate beside him. The other methodically emptied the contents of the canteen over him. Then they left.

He did not mind the drops that fell on him, although he was wet through. Nothing mattered. All living seemed over. He wished only for oblivion.

So the night passed. He could hear the sentries talking and see them lighting pipes in their cupped hands. The mumble of white voices came unintelligibly floating to him like the hungry rumblings of his own stomach, for despite the resolution of his mind and heart, his body still yearned for life. So many of his warriors were dead it seemed improper still to be alive. It would not be for long. He felt sure they would hang him in the morning. White Bird had been right. No matter. He looked once more at the open flap. Stars glittered icily in the pure, wind-whipped sky. From sheer exhaustion, he eventually slept.

He awoke cold and numb. Through his restless sleep he had felt a dull hurt. Now he did not open his eyes, although he realized he was tied hand and foot and some soldiers were standing over him. Once again an interpreter asked him to surrender.

"You have Joseph already. Hang him," he replied.

"Will you surrender the tribe?"

"What terms will you give them?"

The interpreter conferred with an officer.

"Surrender first. Then talk."

"Hang Joseph. Let the people go, and hang me," he told them.

So they hauled him to his feet, cut away the bonds, and marched him out. There was nothing here from which a man might hang. Perhaps they would shoot him. That would be better. Instead, they marched him to the middle ground between the two camps. Even through the blanket, he could feel the muzzle of a gun in his back. Nez Percé with a white officer were approaching from the Indian side. The Indians all had carbines leveled on their captive, a Lieutenant Jovel Jerome, whom they had seized the instant Joseph had been betrayed.

In this way, the exchange was made. Nothing was accomplished by it.

Toward evening, General Howard arrived with his column. Presently another white flag appeared, this time on the Army's side. A treaty Nez Percé, Captain John, whom Joseph's people knew as Jokais, meaning "lazy," bore the truce banner uncertainly. He had come with Howard. Now, in his white man's hat which bore jauntily in the band a last feathered trace of his Indian ancestry, he came to Joseph offering Howard's terms.

"There will be no trials," he said. "No executions. You must surrender. Then they will take you to the Tongue River for the winter."

"Will they leave us rifles for hunting?"

"Enough."

"And ponies? My people will die without their horses."

"You will have enough to hunt. Not to escape."

"Will we go home to the Wallowa?"

"One day you will all go home. General Howard has pledged it."

This was better news than they had hoped, if one could believe it. Joseph gathered his warriors for a last council. Their clothes were torn and filthy, their feet for the most part bare, their eyes red from gunpowder and exhaustion.

"I trust One-Armed Howard more than most men. Without ponies the women and children and the wounded cannot go to the Land of the Old Queen." Silently they heard him out in the makeshift lodge, where the air was blurred with greasy smoke and the snowflakes drifted through the smoke hole and fell into the small fire with little hisses. The even voice went on, telling how it must end. No longer was there hope that the Sioux would come. A wounded grandmother had returned. She had told how the Milk River Sioux had attacked the pack train for the supplies. "A few braves may yet be able to escape," Joseph admitted. "I will hold no one. but I cannot leave those who must stay. My warriors, hear me. Even brave men must surrender when there is nothing else to do. I believe in my heart what General Howard has promised. I am tired of fighting.

Looking Glass is dead. Toohoolhoolzote is dead. All the old men are dead. It is the young men who must decide. Ollokot, who led the young men, is dead. The days grow cold. We have no blankets. Some of our people have run away to the hills. They may be freezing to death. I want time to look for my children and see how many I can save. Hear me, my braves. I am tired. My heart is sick and sad. From where the sun now stands in the sky, I will fight no more forever."

No one else spoke. Joseph stood still as stone. It was over. The earth was strangely silent. Some would hate him. A few might praise him. Ollokot would have understood.

The sun rolled low over the prairie. A small black pony had already been fitted with a Mexican saddle. A chief dressed in his best when meeting with generals. Joseph wore a slate-gray woolen shirt and blanket of red, yellow, and blue. Both shirt and leggings had been torn by bullets. His moccasins were beadless and his braided hair was tied back with a strip of otter fur. His crossed hands held a carbine on the saddle pommel. His head was bowed. He could scarcely feel his body, scarcely tell where it ended and where the cold afternoon air began. The scars on his forehead and wrist were cold as ice.

Slowly he rode up the slope south of the camp toward the flag and the blue soldiers in their heavy warm coats. Big men they were, full of salt pork and beans. Five braves followed him on foot. Their eyes were too dry for tears, but they pressed close around him, their blankets pulled up high in mourning. All were afraid, but they were touched with dignity. Finally, the gun cradled under his arm, Joseph stepped to the ground. He still stood straight and proud, but with a desolation in his eyes. This was the end. He went first to General Howard, whom he knew, but Howard waved him aside to Colonel Miles. Joseph held out his gun, a last abandoning of hope. Miles took it. In silence Joseph drew his blanket over his head. This was the end of the trail. All was over, all but the long dying.

XIII
No Promised Land

Into that featureless plain, white with snow except where the wind had blown bare the hillocks, congregated the Nez Percé. They were blank-eyed, waiting for his sign. Joseph could offer them only the captive's trail through wilderness where dry wind sang under a sky like lead.

The troopers sat in their saddles and stared as though they beheld a side show. Women and old men, hollow-eyed, hollow-cheeked, in ragged shreds of buckskin—was this the Indian army they had fought so long and so hard? Only seventy-nine braves were there. The rest had escaped with a few women and children to Canada. Some Crees and halfbloods had befriended the escapees, as had some of the Sioux. If they had not misread the hand signs, the Sioux would have come to Joseph's aid. They had thought his last stand was on the Missouri River far away.

Two days later, the Nez Percé were moving toward the Missouri. Colonel Miles led the slow column on the six-day march to its banks. This was a Roman triumph for Nelson Miles, and he had the look of a conqueror, with his high cheekbones and deceptively sleepy eyelids. Miles was one who had never flinched at fulfilling his dream: the stars of a general. He already felt warmly toward his prisoners, who, having been defeated at his hands, better served his dream than his rivals in command. Now that the Nez Percé were at his mercy, he felt merciful. He intended to keep all his promises. But there were many wounded, and medical supplies had run out during the battle. The army ambulance wagon could accommodate only two privates, one of whom died on route. Smaller wagons carried injured troopers. During the six-day march to the Missouri, the Indian wounded were dragged on makeshift travois.

The Nez Percé made no attempt to escape. They walked in single file, looking neither to right nor to left at the soldiers. Once on the trail, the cavalry swung into line behind them. At first the weather was clear and cold—good riding weather—and the troopers were glad to be going home. Their thoughts were on warm fires, whiskey, and women left behind. They sang happily . . .

> "Perhaps she's dead, perhaps she's not,
> Perhaps she's on the sea,
> Perhaps she's gone with Brigham Young,
> A Mormon wife to be."

Though a few of the Indians clung to the idea that they were going home with honor, the thoughts of most were melancholy. In sadness they sang their mourning song, not only for the dead and missing, but for the old ways and the land they knew was lost.

On the third day came thunder and lightning, followed by incessant, drenching rain. It was still raining when they reached the banks of the Missouri, and it was there that their position as prisoners was made clear. They did not head southwest for the Wallowa as many had expected, but southeast, following the Yellowstone toward Fort Buford and Bismarck. The wounded and some of the women and children rode the river in open Mackinaw boats. The weather had cleared, but it was very cold. At Bismarck, a crowd awaited them. With flags unfurled, a band, dreadfully out of key, struck up "Hail to the Chief." Colonel Miles sat stiff and erect in his saddle. It was a tune that often played in his head. But this music was for Joseph, and some cheered as he passed by. Their ragged clothes streaming in the wind gave the Nez Percé an odd carnival air, an effect rendered the more bizarre by their hollow faces, masks of death-like indifference. The band, the white people watching, the flags, might have been invisible, so little did the Indians notice them. Joseph, looking only from the corner of his eye, wondered at the spectators and what was written in their faces. Hatred? Pity? Perhaps, along with a cold curiosity about suffering. For the most part, the men were silent. The women whispered together.

While in Bismarck, Joseph received the following formal invitation from the *Tri-Weekly Tribune:* "Sir: Desiring to show you our kind feelings and the admiration we have for your bravery and humanity, as exhibited in your recent conflict with the forces of the United States, we most cordially invite you to dine with us at the Sheridan House in this city. The dinner is to be given at 1:30 P.M. today." No time was allowed for a polite R.S.V.P. Joseph was, after all, a prisoner, and he attended the banquet with a few of his braves. Reporters were present, along with all the "best people." It was better than a medicine show. Colonel Miles made a speech about justice to the Indian, and told how he intended to take Joseph to Washington and insure fair treatment. Joseph comprehended little of this. The room was hot and noisy, and the translator presently became intoxicated. The faces told him nothing at all, the words very little: "I can't tell one Indian from another" . . . "I never saw anybody look so down without it plumb making you feel uncomfortable." They were speaking about him, that much Joseph knew. Louder, he thought, if only they would speak louder. They were speaking loudly enough. He just couldn't understand the words.

At Bismarck a second pledge to the Nez Percé, one never seriously intended, was broken. The tribe was separated from the last few ponies before being marched on foot to the railroad station. Their bones jutted out. Their eyes were black holes. Some trotted to get warm. There were no bands this time, and no large crowds. A few local Indians in embroidered buckskin, thoroughly domesticated and dignified as Roman senators, watched them board in terror the eleven mud-spattered, smoke-blackened coaches that would carry them south to Fort Leavenworth in Kansas.

Joseph was the last to board. He took leave of Colonel Miles, who had pledged so much through an interpreter. "You could have shown me your true intention," Joseph said. "It is all around you like a cloud. It is what you are planning all the time when you are talking about anything else. I would call you friend, but where is our land? I would call you brother, but where are my horses? If you spoke true, I would never have surrendered."

Colonel Miles stared at the sky. Then he took a deep breath and looked Joseph in the eye. "You and your people would all be dead if you had not surrendered. You were wise to surrender."

"Are we not dead? Who tells me we are not dead now?" Joseph asked him.

"I am not finished with Washington," the Colonel told him. "Believe me, Joseph, I am not finished." But as far as Joseph was concerned, the sun had been put out. There was cold comfort in the moon.

Joseph said no more. Perhaps the mistake of his life had been to talk. A shout came from the engine, which leaped forward as if to snap the cars in two. Indians sprawled in the aisles. With the whuff-whuff of tired steam, the train gained momentum. It stopped once for water and fuel, then ground on through the night, a great snake with a fiery head, winding through the winter night. All the next day the train passed over rivers and through gaps in the hills with the grinding of wheels and the exhausted breathing of the engine. The silvery mountains faded into the hard sky. Joseph thought of home. That was gone. Freedom was gone. Many were dead, but as long as he had his wife and little daughter, it would not be entirely the white man's hell. A child said something about a man—that he had existed. Then, at a water stop not far north of Fort Leavenworth, Joseph was given a chance to stretch his legs and he was left thoughtfully pacing the tracks. When the train began to move, he shouted for it to stop. No one noticed him. The guards who had fought so hard to imprison him had their backs turned. Slowly, then with increasing speed, the train pulled away. He was free, but in freedom nothing remained without his people. Still shouting, Joseph ran down the track. The ground seemed to rise and fall beneath him. Things took on strange colors. He ran steadily for an hour until there was nothing real but pain. When the error was discovered, and after an alarm for an escaped renegade had been telegraphed from the next station, the train came huffing back. It seemed miles off to Joseph, floating in a mist. Staggering, his lungs wheezing with exhaustion, he allowed himself to be hauled back into captivity.

In the deserts of a foreign land, the Nez Percé were nothing. Joseph felt them to be infinitesimal and forgotten, driven along strange trails where they no longer could hear the warrior's song. Yet they were his people, and they were all that mattered. Particularly the children, for the old had had their years, which could not be stolen. The young might have their lives taken from them. He must be as a light for them, as long as he lived, to make safe the darkness in which they must live.

The Nez Percé spent the balance of the winter as prisoners at Fort Leavenworth. In the spring, when mosquitoes rose from the malarial swamps, they began to sicken and die. From the prison, Joseph made his first appeal for justice, a petition for removal north, which General Sherman, as final military authority, disapproved. He believed in dead Indians. In July, jurisdiction over the Nez Percé passed from the Army to the Indian Bureau, and the tribe was removed by wagon to Indian territory. The Indians already there called it Eeikish Pah, the hot place. By midsummer the last moisture in the dry Oklahoma land had escaped into the sky. The sun and the restless breezes drew up only dust, which coated the sagebrush, the canvas tipis, and the beasts that moved through shimmering waves of heat. To the Nez Percé, accustomed to mountains and pine forests and salmon-filled streams, it was a land without substance or beauty.

They were told it would be the sort of home they made of it. If they were lazy and did not work with the pick and hoe, their crops would not grow. Some roamed, looking for deer. Others lay all day under the canvas. A few planted seeds, but there was no crop and little game, and whatever they did, they died of the yellow vomit. No longer enemies of the white man, they seemed scarcely to be creatures of this earth, only blanketed shadows of starvation and malaria. By October, when the heat began to break, one out of every five Nez Percé was dead. Among the first to die was Daytime Smoke, the aged half-breed son of Captain William Clark. The circle of injustice was complete. The Nez Percé were almost forgotten.

But not entirely. General Howard, who derived more ridicule than glory from the Nez Percé campaign, washed his hands of the whole affair. Colonel Nelson Miles had come away with the glory, and with respect for a people who could hold off two thousand regulars and volunteers in a 1,700-mile retreat involving four battles and countless skirmishes. He had boundless admiration for Joseph, who had moved throughout victory and final defeat with all the dignity of a hero in classic tragedy. In January 1879, through Miles's efforts, Joseph was called to Washington, where he addressed both Congress and Cabinet. His voice is preserved out of the hundreds that were silenced. He alone told how the Nez Percé had lived and hoped and attempted to preserve their way of life, how they had failed and died.

"If the white man wants to live in peace with the Indian, he can live in peace. There need be no trouble. Treat all men alike. Give them all the same law. Give them all an even chance to live and grow. All men were made by the same Great Spirit Chief. They are all brothers. The earth is the mother of all people, and all people should have equal rights upon it. You might as well expect the rivers to run backward as that any man who was born free should be contented penned up and denied liberty to go where he pleases. Let me be a free man, free to travel, free to stop, free to work, free to trade, where I choose, free to choose my own teachers, free to follow the religion of my fathers, free to think and talk and act for myself—and I will obey every law, or submit to the penalty." His voice alone outlasts time.

Washington listened, but took no action. Joseph returned to Indian territory and his people, who sang a new song of better days left behind. They went on about the business of dying. In Joseph's family, the baby, barely able to toddle on spidery bowlegs, was the first to go. Spring Song, found as a slave among the Sioux in Canada, had been returned. Her eyes peered out from dark hollows. Her lips were blue and sunken, like the toothless mouth of an old woman. The Sioux had broken her. She would not speak of it. She would not speak at all. When the malaria came, she seemed to welcome it and died. Singing Beads became ill at the same time. The fever imposed an animal mask upon her once lovely face. She did not wish to leave Joseph and there was a hurt in her eyes, like a child who is punished without explanation. "Why . . . why . . . why . . ." Joseph held her head in his lap all that last night. He could not give an answer. Toward morning she, too, was dead, and he was alone.

The emptiness was a black abyss at his feet into which he would gladly step but for his people. There was no mystery about Joseph. He was simply a man who was bound to his tribe. Something inside him made him carry on their living, go on with it when they no longer cared and he, too, wanted to give up. That was the most frightening part of it, no longer caring. Some did not even remember how it had once been.

In 1881, Miles, a general at last, appealed to President Hayes. By 1883 the Nez Percé had become a national issue. Two years later, 188 survivors were sent north, not to the Wallowa but to the Lapwai Reservation. There White Bird, who had skulked in Canada, rejoined them. The rest, including Joseph and those braves against whom indictments remained on the dockets of the Idaho courts, were sent to the Colville Reservation in the state of Washington. Not a child born in Oklahoma went with them, for not one had survived.

In 1889, when Joseph was offered removal to Lapwai, he declined. Through the years he fought for a return to the Wallowa. He remained tall and dignified, but something more than his youth was gone. His authority was that of a captive who rules other captives. Not until 1900 was he able to visit the Wallowa with James McLaughlin, the Indian agent. They went by way of Lapwai, and Joseph could smell the town from a mile away. It drove out the scent of the woods—stale beer, cheap whiskey, spoiled meat. There the Indians lived like badgers, their holes ringed with rubbish and rusting tools. He had seen Washington, D.C., all cement and brick piling up. He had seen the bench with wheels. How long until the trees, the surge of a good horse, would be forgotten forever?

"I don't know these people," he said.

So they rode out to the Wallowa in the hope of obtaining a small reservation for the survivors of Joseph's tribe. Here, too, the wilderness had withdrawn from the valley as before a tide. The plow and the double-edged ax and the miner's pick, more than the soldier's gun, had driven out the Indians and the animals who had haunted the wilds. White men and women, with mule teams and young children, had replaced the hunters and trappers who once lived with and accepted the Indians. They had made the land their own. No longer content with log cabins, they were the builders of roads and towns, the diggers of mines, people who not only fished for salmon but canned what they caught.

They wanted no Indians on their land, these men who could hardly remember a drunken Indian in the local jail. There was no place for Joseph and his people here.

Like a tourist in a foreign land, Joseph visited the old haunts and the new monuments. "Before you to the westward lies the historic White Bird Battleground of the Nez Percé Indian War in which thirty-four men gave their lives in the service of their country, June 17, 1877. Beneath this shaft lies one of these men who rests where he fell." No mention in marble of the Indians who fought for their homeland.

When the last hope of obtaining land had been exhausted, Joseph asked whether he might visit his father's grave in the Wallowa. Surprisingly, the homesteader who owned the land had kept the grave carefully intact. With evident pride, he led Joseph to the spot. Apart from the missing tokens which had once hung there, it was the same, and Joseph stood for some time in silence. Then he gazed off at the mountains. They were the same sharp peaks, the same rolled thunderheads. But inside him all the years piled up and the dream was dead in his eyes. At least there was some small comfort in knowing that his father's remains had been protected. He would never know that the homesteader, together with a visiting dentist, had dug up and removed Old Joseph's skull some years before to adorn the dentist's waiting room.

So Joseph returned to Colville. He was old. There was nothing more he could do. He made no further appeals.

His last public appearance was July 4, 1904. He was a harmless institution by that time—obsolete. It didn't even matter whether he or his few remaining people resented their lot. Within a few more years, the last of them would disappear. It was a white man's land, and so they took the old chief out on Independence Day and told him to stand for his photograph. They put a war bonnet on his head, which he had never worn, and a brass-framed Winchester in his hand. The photographer urged him to smile, but Indians never smiled for their pictures and Joseph was still an Indian with deep, sad eyes that looked older than one man's lifetime. He was a dignified man still, and he stood over six feet tall, straight as a ridgepole pine. His neck was thick and strong, though eroded into fissures by the years, and only when he shut his eyes did the life go out of his face.

When the pictures were over, the photographer handed him several coins. They bore the portrait of an Indian, and he wondered if by some magic they had come from the camera. In years gone by, he might have thrown the money on the ground, but he was past that sort of foolish pride, and the coins would pay for tobacco. For a moment he hesitated, not knowing whether the pictures were over. Then he left, stately and yet forlorn, looking as though no one owned him. He headed for his lodge. The summer sun did not seem as warm as it used to be.

The lodge was his last refuge. He dwelt there amid old things—trade blankets, baskets woven by Singing Beads, a pipe tomahawk with the dull edge of a reservation toy. He had never wielded such a thing in battle or in sport, but he smoked it now.

There was comfort in the sweet inner bark of the red willow, mixed with the dried sumac leaves. There was even a kind of contentment in being in the darkness, alone, without anyone needing him. The smoke rose slowly as he tried to recall through its haze a green glade backed by woods with horses running free. It was better to have had the Wallowa once and to have lost it than never to have known it at all. He no longer sang the sorrow song for those days. It did not even run through his head. There was no song left in him. Only a numbness and the memory, for his heart had shrunken in him, and he kept only the past like bits of a broken clay pot.

He looked at his hands, waiting for the old thoughts to begin. In the wreathing smoke, he saw it only faintly at first, the Wallowa. The name for him had a singing sound, ringing softly and sadly inside his head: Wallowa, an echo of itself. He seldom dreamed now of great deeds or of fighting the troopers. He did not dream of Singing Beads or his children, only of the Wallowa: the light on the lake water and the deer coming down to drink, the quiet trips along the bending river and the wide meadows with horses grazing.

With tips from a photographer and from an occasional tourist, Joseph bought tobacco to smoke away that last summer of 1904 until the aspens changed to gold and the nights were cold, tasting of the snow to come. All those years ago, he'd been at the foot of the

Bear Paw Mountains at this time of year. The memory tried to intrude on his happier recollections and then, clear as spring water, he saw Ollokot, his brother. For a moment his head reeled as the lean dark figure strode toward him, bringing back days when the world was carefree and young. The figure held up a bit of sparkling green glass. He dreamed of Spring Song, too, in that cat nap of old age. "Spring Song." He said her name aloud, and with this she vanished like a string of broken pearls. Singing Beads, and with her the baby, rose as from dark waters. Behind them shimmered the ranks of his people, the Nez Percé, those who would not be tamed. They had what the world had lost, a power to live and a lost reverence and a passion for the earth and its web of life. In his mind Joseph led them again into the flung snow, moving always north toward freedom. They called to him through the thunder and the singing wind. He had heard that cry before, long and high and sorrowful. Someone was in pain. A little wrinkled strain came between his brows. Somewhere he was needed, and Joseph braced himself to help. His knee joints cracked as he stood up, but Joseph did not hear them. He heard only the victim's cry, the voice of his people. The arrow that had lodged between his ribs so long now took a last turn. But it wasn't an arrow any more. It was an eagle taking flight.

On September 21, 1904, the body of Chief Joseph was found slumped before the ashes of his lodge fire. The Colville agency physician came round in the morning and reported only that he had died of a broken heart.

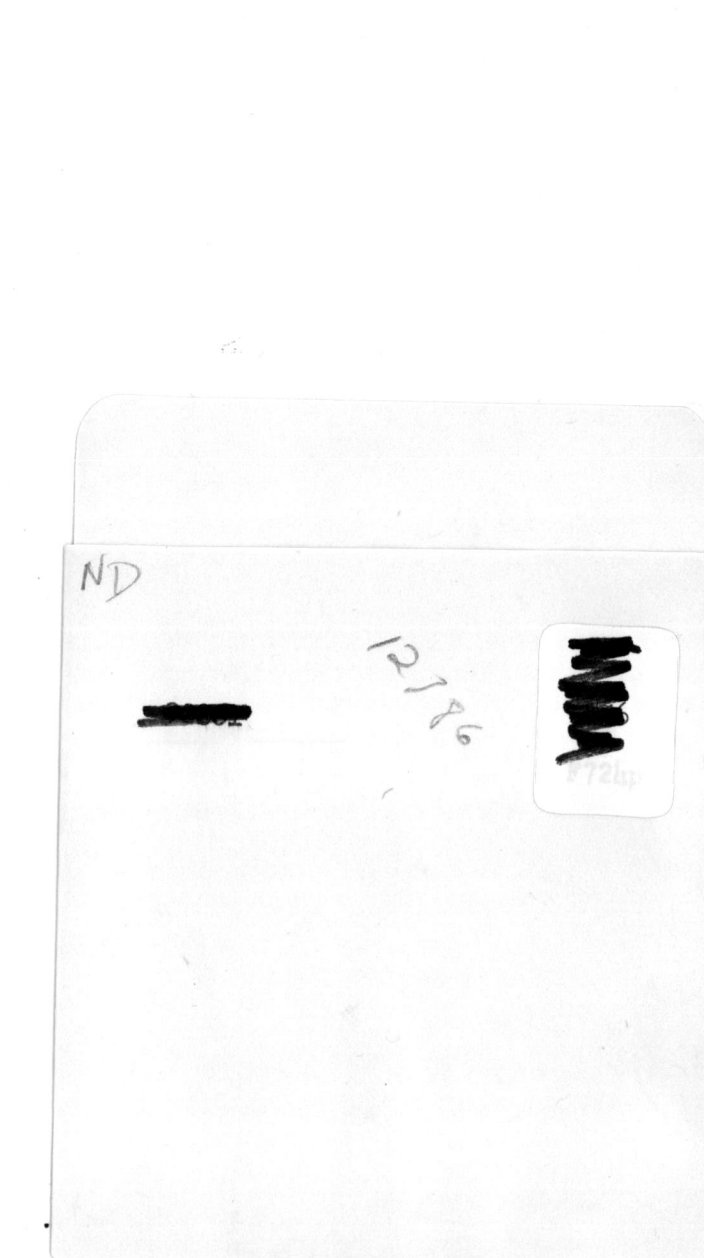

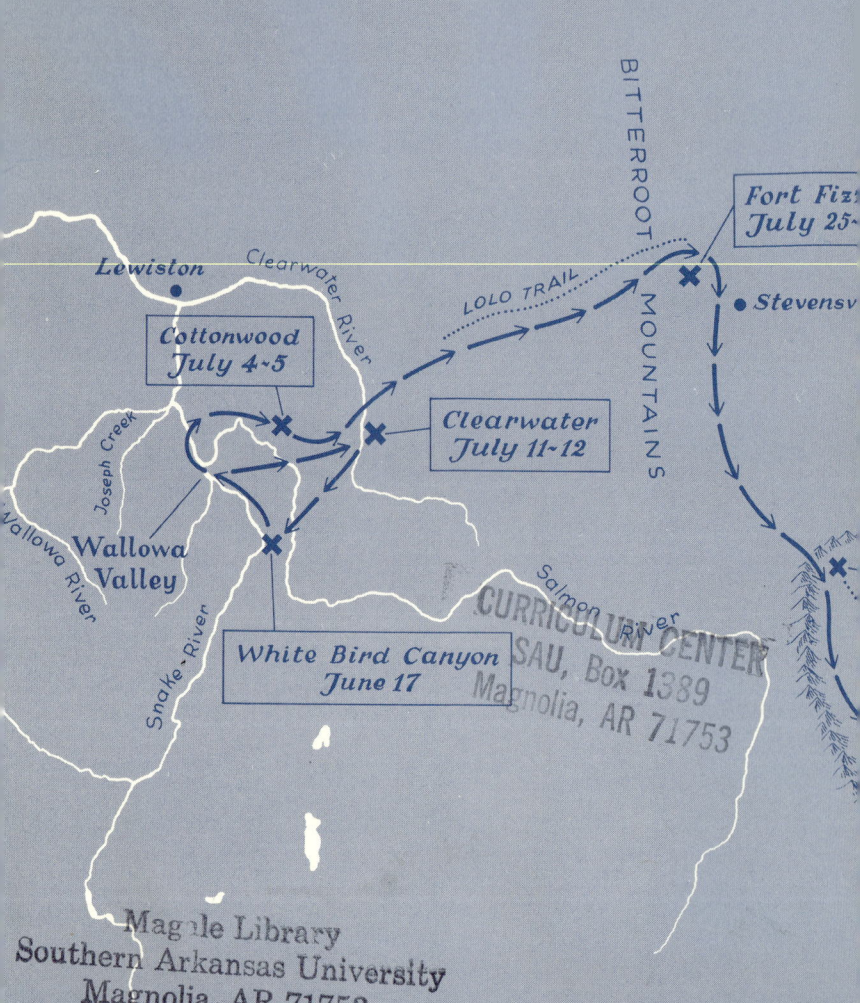